Praise for *Town Kid*

"Want to learn what a 1950s boyhood was like in Greenfield, Iowa—population 2,000? Read Gary Porter's wonderful new book, *Town Kid*. You'll visit the Grand Theater, the Carnegie Library, Rexall Drugstore, and St. John's Catholic Church. And you'll even become acquainted with the dreaded pool hall—off limits to kids Porter's age—and much more."

Jerry Apps, Author of *Simple Things:*
Lessons from the Family Farm

"My ol' pal and hero-in-journalism Hugh Sidey once led off a *Time* magazine column by saying, 'When I think of my childhood in Greenfield, Iowa, I can't remember ever being bored, not ever, not a single time.' It was that way for Hugh when he grew up there in the 1930s and 40s, and this new book of essays by Gary Porter proves it was still that way for his generation of Greenfield kids in the 1950s and 60s. It's high praise for a town if people grow up and grow old thinking that way."

Chuck Offenburger, Former "Iowa Boy"
Columnist, *Des Moines Register*

"Rich with sensory detail and evocative memories, *Town Kid* is a delightful collection of essays that together form a love story about small-town life in the 1960s. You don't have to be from Greenfield or Iowa to enjoy Porter's trip down memory lane."

Carol Bodensteiner, Author of
Growing Up Country: Memories of an Iowa Farm Girl

"*Town Kid* defines 'home' with amusing and heartfelt stories of the author's youth, which prompts a flood of wonderful memories. The magic lies in the ability of the stories to transport us back to our own youth."

John H. Potter, Executive Director,
The Phipps Center for the Arts

"Who needs H.G. Wells and his time machine when you've got Gary Porter's stories? Warm and heartfelt reminiscences about a time that you lived in or now wish you had."

Brian Roegge, Owner, Chapter2Books

"When Gary asked me to work with him, using The Sidey Collection® for his new book, I thought, *What fun!* And it was fun...and a great way to showcase photos by the Sidey journalists. Some were taken by K. H. Sidey; others by my husband, Ed; and highly likely some by interns and staff. Gary was very selective and made sure the photos fit his vision. I hope Gary continues to record his thoughts and memories and that The Sidey Collection is included in them. Thanks, Gary!"

Linda Sidey, The Sidey Collection

TOWN
KID

TOWN KID

Reflections of a Midwestern Boyhood

GARY PORTER

PUBLISHING + DESIGN

ISBN: 978-0-9994887-8-2

Library of Congress Control Number: 2018955888

Published and printed in the United States of America by the Write Place, Inc. For more information, please contact:

the Write Place, Inc.
809 W. 8th Street, Suite 2
Pella, Iowa 50219
www.thewriteplace.biz

Cover and interior design by Michelle Stam, the Write Place, Inc.
Cover photo courtesy of The Sidey Collection®.
Cover quote: Hugh Sidey, *Adair County Free Press*, Sept. 11, 2002.

Copies of this book may be ordered online at Amazon and BarnesandNoble.com.

View other Write Place titles at www.thewriteplace.biz.

DEDICATION

For Melissa,
the love of my life for forty years.

To the memory of Bob Timbers,
a kind and gentle soul.

REFLECTIONS

FOREWORD

At sixty-one, I am still unabashedly passionate about my summers in Iowa. Some of my most vivid memories come to life and transport me back to the spirited freedom of summers past.

The warm breezes of August feather my skirt and dust over my cotton top as I float down the Midway at the Adair County Fair in Greenfield, Iowa. Sights and sounds capture my thoughts with each step as I move farther into the glow of the evening—the whole of my senses awakened by the familiarity of many summers spent in the heart of the prairie.

I smile and tilt my head with abandon. They call me a "city slicker" since I live on the East Coast. But the summers of my late teens in Greenfield are very much still in my mind's eye. The memories pop up often enough to fondly remind me what it was like to be nineteen and without a care in the world, living the small-town dream.

There are no places so welcome as those I remember from the summers of my youth. Gary Porter's *Town Kid: Reflections of a Midwestern Boyhood* has captured much of this longing.

Town Kid is a sentimental journey, beautifully written and justly deserving of praise and appreciation. Porter's style is much like that of a storyteller; his essays are fluid and vulnerable, provocative and romantic. A favorite author of Porter's, Mark Twain, once said, "Write what your heart tells you." In this collection of essays, Porter gently reminds us that the beauty and simplicity in our hearts is just a memory away.

Cynthia Sidey Buck
July 19, 2018

NOTICE TO THE READER

One of my favorite authors is the man in the white suit from Hannibal, Missouri: Samuel Clemens. Riverboat pilot, prospector, newspaper man. Eventually he took the pen name Mark Twain, arguably the most recognized name in the world at one time.

Four of Mark Twain's classics—including *The Adventures of Huckleberry Finn* and *The Adventures of Tom Sawyer*—are prized possessions, treasures from my childhood that are prominently displayed on one of our many bookcases. In addition to penning these timeless novels, Mr. Clemens had plenty to say on a variety of other topics, including how to write your life story. One of his notions was that a writer should not *publish* an autobiography until he was deceased, reasoning that only from the grave would he be "dead, and unaware, and indifferent." He might *write* his story prior to passing—this would seem to be a necessity, would it not—but the story would not be published until he was on the other side. In fact, in Twain's estimation a period of one hundred years would be a reasonable passage of time before publication.

I am pleased to report that I am certainly not dead—not just yet anyway—and hopefully neither unaware nor indifferent, although both of these traits are certainly subjective in nature and open to argument. So, on the one hand, I cast aside the advice of this trusted sage and at great risk not only write my story, but throw it out there for public consumption. But if I were to try to somehow justify this premature publication, I would say that what follows is not autobiographical in nature. In fact, it is decidedly not my *life's* story. I would argue that a life that now spans more than six decades is far too lengthy to fit into a single volume. The cynic would argue a different but maybe even more compelling point: What could be *that* interesting about the life of a person trained in the practice of accounting, as I was many years ago at Drake University?

So instead of a true autobiography, I have chosen here to focus on my pre-bean-counting years—before I went off to college, before I knew the difference between a debit and a credit, and certainly prior to any notion that I could earn a salary by teaching others the difference between the two.

Another of Mark Twain's thoughts about writing a life story was that it should follow no chronological order, but rather "start at no particular time of your life; wander at your free will all over your life."

My reflections here follow a similar pattern of randomness, proceeding in no particular chronological order and wandering freely as I see fit. My thinking is that if it was good enough for Mark Twain it is good enough for me. After all, how could one start in true chronological order, at the date of one's entry into this world? There is no denying I was present at the time and place of my birth, but as any truth-telling person would admit, I have no recollection of the blessed event. I don't recall being slapped on the posterior by the delivering physician, although I know this was standard practice at the time. Nor do I recall what I was wearing, although I have been told it was the standard dress for the day, that being a birthday suit.

It is interesting to ask people what their absolute earliest recollections are about their lives. Some are honest, while others would lead you to believe they remember the ride home from the hospital. *It was a hot, sultry summer morning, long before air conditioning. Dad set me down on the car seat between him and Mom, years before baby seats or seat belts. He rolled down the windows and off we went, jarring along on the dusty gravel roads that covered the five miles to home.* Such nonsense—no one remembers that far back.

Myself, I go back to kindergarten with Miss Edna Huston, in the ancient brick edifice on the south side of town—a building that a few years later would be home to the junior high. Kindergarten was a half day then. Linus-like, I carried a blanket to school for the requisite nap taken on a ledge in a room on the north side of the main floor. The name of the teacher, the location, the siesta, and my accompaniment—that's about the extent of my remembering. I have no recollection of first grade. I pick up my recollections in second grade.

So, in keeping with the advice of one of my literary heroes, I choose to start at no particular time and wander at my free will. But I do my wandering from this side of the grave, where I hope to remain for many years to come.

PROLOGUE

The memory is a curious thing, to be trusted one day and driven out the next, banned from our bodies and souls. Trusted to recall some of the happiest times in our lives, however we may choose to define them. Driven out when we are reminded of the depths of our existence, when loved ones are lost and our faith in humanity is tested.

But in reality, none of us choose what to remember or what to forget. That would be too easy, too self-serving. Unfortunately, we are only the repositories for that other voice in our heads, the one telling us what we do and don't remember.

Memories trick us, like passing clouds in an otherwise brilliant sky. They shift, they change shape, they pass by, they fade out. Eventually most memories disappear, leaving only that bright blue sky. A few do keep their shape, refusing to fade away. It's the senses that resist, wanting to hold on to the sights and sounds of that summer day from so many years ago. That cloudless morning when neither yesterday nor tomorrow mattered to a young boy.

Only what today would hold.

PART I

Living

Courtesy of The Sidey Collection®

As a town kid in the fifties, I can't recall ever looking backward to yesterday or forward to tomorrow. There was never time for such introspection. There was a world to explore, even if it was a patch of ground no more than a mile in any one direction.

Beyond the obvious difference in the physical layout of our commercial districts—mine a square, his a Main Street—the hometown of my youth bore little resemblance to that of Sinclair Lewis. His fictional town was filled with grief, conflict, cynicism, and jealousies. Maybe when left to their own devices the adults in my town concerned themselves with such trivialities, but they didn't exist in the mind of a young boy.

Not to say my hometown was the sort of place imagined by Mark Twain. There may have been a streak of Huck Finn or Tom Sawyer in some of us, but we had no rivers to escape down. We were landlocked. We found our adventures in the alleys, in the open fields, in the playgrounds around town. This is where we did our living.

Personal Collection

TOWN KID

*"The 1950s and 1960s saw a
Rockwellian version of American life."*

From "History" on www.greenfieldiowa.com

We all get the question, *Where are you from?* Without hesitation I proudly proclaim, *Iowa!* Iowa, land of the tall corn, *Field of Dreams*, and *The Bridges of Madison County*. The state sandwiched between the two great rivers, the Missouri and the Mississippi. Invariably, the follow-up question to the first is, *So, you grew up on a farm?*

The assumption is that if you hail from Iowa you must have been a farm kid. You must know about corn and soybean yields, crop rotation, and market prices for yearling heifers. The blank look on my face answers no, I didn't grow up on a farm. Finally, the interrogator asks, *So what* town *was it that you grew up in?* The assumption is that all outposts of civilization in Iowa could only qualify as towns, certainly not deserving of city status. Tongue in cheek, I answer, *I grew up in the suburbs.*

According to Webster, a suburb is a district near the outskirts of a city. Our house sat on the north side of Greenfield, Iowa, population 2,000. Two thousand when I was growing up in the fifties and sixties and 2,000 today. Certainly not the same 2,000 for all these years, but when I left home for college in 1968 someone moved to town to take my place. And now when someone dies, either at the hospital on the edge of town—as my mom did—or at the nursing home next door—as my dad did—a baby is born to take their place.

The hospital has served the good citizens of Greenfield since 1950, the year of my entrance into the world. I was in fact the third baby born in the Adair County Memorial Hospital. Prior to that, the mothers in town had to make a road trip of twenty miles to Creston to deliver their babies. It came to my attention, many years later of course, that there was quite a celebration when the new hospital opened, and that they showered gifts on the first baby born there. I loved to tease Mom about this. Why couldn't she have sped things up just a bit? Why did she have to wait until September 8, 1950, rather than say September 1, 1950? Think of the haul we could have taken in, not to mention the fame the two of us could have achieved! She'd just give me that wink of hers as she reached to light up a Parliament and take a sip from her ever-present coffee cup.

Our neighbors to the north, the Galbreaths, had a barn we rented to stable our horses. Across the road, farther north from the Galbreaths, was a working farm owned by the Bartletts, where we walked for eggs and cream. So there I was, residing on the outskirts of a city—okay, a town—which must have qualified me as a suburbanite.

Tongue out of my cheek, I was a town kid through and through. From my vantage point on that northern edge of Greenfield, I could see the whole town. It was my playground. I was Opie, and Greenfield was a Midwestern cousin to Mayberry. Granted, my dad wasn't sheriff, as Opie's was. But my *grandpa* was the sheriff of Adair County back in the early part of the twentieth century. He died the year before I was born.

Directly across the street from our house was the swimming pool. From as far back as my memory serves me, I spent the hot, sultry days of summer at the swimming pool. Long before daycare, the pool was our babysitter from sunup to sundown. The public grounds around the pool were our own private ball fields, used for pickup baseball games in the spring and summer and tackle football in the fall and sometimes right into winter. The baseball and football games started out differently—the former involving a batter, a pitcher, and fielders, the latter a passer, blockers, and tacklers. At some point though, both games ended up pretty much the same: a tangle of arms and legs piled on top of each other. Throw a Band-Aid on any open wounds and off we went to the cooling waters of the pool.

Adjacent to the pool, and just a stone's throw from our house on Dodge Street, sat St. John's Catholic Church. Mom, a Fagan by birth and Irish by blood, was a staunch Catholic. Dad was the son of Protestant parents, Methodists to be specific. There was never any doubt how my brother John and I would be raised, learning to genuflect at a young age.

Even though we attended the public school—our parish was too small to support its own school—so much of our education took place at St. John's. Officially, Father Bartholomew Kane was the parish priest, but his influence was much more far reaching. Not always successful in his efforts, he tried his hardest to expand our horizons. Beyond the requisite Latin needed to serve as altar boys, he tried to teach us other languages, such as Spanish and French. Many a day was spent in the tiled-floor church basement as he worked to educate us, with a bottle of 7 Up the reward for our efforts. Long before it achieved such widespread popularity among kids in this country, he introduced us to the game of soccer, so much a part of the fabric in his native Ireland.

A disproportionate number of my recollections of growing up in Greenfield involve Father Kane and the old church across the street. On a cold winter morning, I could fall out of bed and be in the vestibule of the church in five minutes, putting on my cassock and getting ready to serve seven o'clock Mass.

The city park was two blocks down the street from the pool and the church, and the town square another two blocks farther south. I am not sure what it is about a town square that elicits such memories. But for me, the town kid, that center of commerce will forever be cemented in my mind. Leave it to my hometown to not have the *typical* square. On most town squares, you enter from one of the four corners. Our square begged to be different. On ours, you entered on one of the four streets that brought you directly into the center of the square. Architects call this the Lancaster style. The corners of the square were reserved for alleys, where a person could make a much less ceremonious entrance—say, when that person might be slipping into one of the beer joints that lay on these corners of the square.

Greenfield is the seat of Adair County. The courthouse occupied the middle of the square and was the hub of all of the "official" business in town. For many years, Uncle Max served as the county clerk. There was many a day when my buddies and I would stride up the steps as if we actually had some official business at the courthouse and pop in to say hello to Uncle Max and his assistants.

Stores surrounded the courthouse on all four sides of the square. I use the past tense because many of those stores are long gone, victims of "progress." The stores contained everything you ever needed, or at least wanted: Berg's Sure Save Market, Piper Variety, Heiny's TV and Furniture, Eddie's Super Popcorn, Crooks Clothing, Fry's Rexall Drug. Imagine walking into a Walmart today. The only difference is that back then you walked out the door from one store to the next rather than cruising up and down the aisles of some super center.

The town square was also the center of entertainment, the definition of that term dependent on some combination of your age and religious beliefs. Take the pool hall on the northeast corner of the square. Liquor wasn't sold in the pool hall. It was the smokin', chewin', and language that made it off limits for me by my mother's edict. One thing to learn Latin to say the Mass, another to pick up the vernacular of a pool hall.

The beer joints in town—no lounges or clubs in Greenfield— were beyond mere parental restrictions. They were *legally* off limits until you reached drinking age. Also legally off limits was the peculiar establishment known as the State of Iowa Liquor Store, kitty-corner from the pool hall. In those days the liquor store was where the adults went to buy a fifth of whiskey to take home for that Saturday night highball.

On the other hand, a safe haven at any age was the Grand Theatre. In the days before DVDs, Red Boxes, and home theatres, the Grand *was* our home theatre. Many a Saturday night was spent there with a bag of buttered popcorn and a cup that magically dropped down and filled up with Coke, right before your eyes.

Long before the current PG and R ratings, the screening for what we kids could and couldn't see was provided by the weekly Catholic newspaper. A phone conversation between my mother and her sister, Aunt Blanche, would determine whether we cousins would be seeing that week's picture.

Just off the south side of the square was the Carnegie Library. It looked much like every other library funded by the wealthy philanthropist: a red-brick, rectangular building with large, white frame windows and steep steps leading up to the main floor. Once inside, there was a certain reverence to the place, not unlike that observed at church. When you asked Lalla Cornell, the librarian, for help finding *Robinson Crusoe*, it was with a whisper, nothing louder. You learned the Dewey Decimal System at a young age, searching through the wooden card catalog to find biographies in the 920s for that book report on George Washington. Many a day was spent cruising the aisles, sitting on the floor immersed in other places that were lifetimes and worlds away from our little town.

The house I grew up in is gone, a "teardown" in the language of today's impersonal world. The swimming pool across the street is still there, although our ball fields have been paved over and turned into tennis courts. Old St. John's was leveled many years ago and replaced with a modern, ranch-style building. The parish still goes by the same name, but I don't see St. John's when I drive by now.

The old courthouse still stands in the middle of the town square, although every so often there is some crazy talk about "consolidation" of counties. You can still see a picture at the Grand, but the pool hall is boarded up and the last of the beer joints is gone from the square. You want to shoot a game of eight ball and drink a glass of beer, you go off the square to the bowling alley. The Carnegie is no longer a library. The town's collection of books was moved across the street to a prefab building shared with City Hall.

Not all is gloom and doom. The recently restored Warren Opera House is a treasure for a town of our size. Concerts, plays, dances, and all sorts of entertainment beckon back to the glory days of the place. The old hotel, now called Hotel Greenfield, has also been restored to its original grandeur. The *Adair County Free Press* still faithfully informs and entertains the citizens every Wednesday, as it has in one form or another for over a hundred years. The library may not be a Carnegie, but it is a community treasure, holding as it does the history and stories of our town.

It has been fifty years, half a century, since I left Greenfield to go away to college. I have lived away from my hometown for much longer than I lived in it. But as the name implies, the town is, and forever will be, my home. And for those precious years of my youth, I was a town kid and Greenfield was my town.

Courtesy of The Sidey Collection®

GREENFIELD

*"Greenfield is a thriving little city of wide-awake,
enterprising citizens....The business portion of the town
never appears dull to the observer....Life and property
are valued and well established and maintained, and with
good society, healthy and delightful climate, good location
of the city as to drainage, railroad, telephone, telegraph and
mail facilities, good schools and churches and institutions,
living in Greenfield is a decidedly pleasant occupation."*

From *1915 History of Adair County Iowa and Its People*,
Lucian M. Kilburn, Supervising Editor

So how do you describe the hometown of your youth to a stranger? By its population? The ethnicity of its people? Its weather? Its topography? The rivers that run through it? How many stoplights it has? The number of hotels and restaurants? By the names of the main streets? By the famous people who moved away to achieve fortune and fame somewhere else?

Greenfield, Iowa. Population 2,000. Caucasian. Cold and snowy in the winter, hot and sultry in the summer. Flat in town, rolling hills outside the city limits. No rivers run through town, but out in the country there is the Grand, the Middle, and the Nodaway—creeks generously given the status of rivers. The old lake and the new lake, as they are descriptively called by locals, lie on the outskirts of town, but I never thought of them as being a part of the town itself. They were more like distant cousins. No, Greenfield is a town of the earth, supported as it has been all these years by the fertile fields surrounding its borders.

The closest things to stoplights in Greenfield are the flashing red and yellow lights at the intersection of State Highways 25 and 92 on the east side of town. Otherwise, a few stop signs are placed judiciously around town to slow speeding teenagers bent on pushing the limits.

The one motel in town is now gone and the old hotel has alternated between periods of occupancy and idleness over the years. Recently restored, Hotel Greenfield is now a gem just off the town square. The MaidRite, home of the original loose-meat sandwich (finely crumbled ground beef, pickles, chopped onion, and mustard), is a distant memory. But you can get a hot meal next door to the hotel at the Olive Branch.

Growing up, no one paid any attention to the *names* of streets in Greenfield. Certainly, there were identifiers for the streets, names for the east-west streets and numbers for the north-souths. A few nods to presidents—a Grant Street, a Hayes, a Jackson. Iowa Street took you onto the square. But I don't ever recall my parents telling a relative visiting from out of town, *We live on Dodge Street, between Second and Third Streets.* Even though that is precisely where we lived, at 205 NE Dodge Street.

Say the visitor was coming down State Highway 25, off Interstate 80. *Turn right at the Lutheran church, go a couple blocks until you see the Catholic church on your left, and continue on into the next block. You will see the swimming pool on your left. We're across the street, second house on the right.* Who needs street numbers and names with such precise directions? Sure don't need MapQuest or Google.

Folks in Greenfield never talked about any famous native sons, or daughters for that matter. We were envious to know John Wayne was born in Winterset, our neighbor to the east. Heck, Orient, a speck of a town ten miles south, could claim Henry Wallace, Vice President of the United States. My dad's favorite ball team was the Cleveland Indians, probably because Bob Feller, the towering Hall of Fame fireballer, hailed from Van Meter, which was just down the road from us. Greenfield eventually did have its own celebrity, Hugh Sidey, but it wasn't until after I had left town that Hugh achieved most of his fame as the chronicler of the presidents in *Time* magazine. His brother, Ed, stayed home and ran the *Adair County Free Press* until the day he died.

Even though we couldn't lay claim to any movie stars, Greenfield *itself* achieved celebrity status. It was the summer of 1969. Film director Norman Lear "discovered" Greenfield, as if our town was neatly tucked away in a scrapbook, dusted off, and presented to the public for the first time. Legend has it Mr. Lear travelled the Midwest searching for the quintessential small town in which to film his movie about an entire community that would go "cold turkey," giving up smoking for thirty days in exchange for a healthy sum of money. The movie *Cold Turkey* brought a multitude of stars to town that summer, Dick Van Dyke, Bob Newhart, Jean Stapleton, and Tom Poston among them.

As Hollywood types are wont to do, our town was given a new name. Greenfield became Eagle Rock for the silver screen, and vestiges of that name are still scattered about town on a few signs built for the movie sets. There was a world premiere at the

Grand and locals nudged each other to point out a relative or friend making a cameo appearance.

Our town returned to normal after its summer in the sun. Eagle Rock transformed back into Greenfield. Nothing flashy about that name. Not compared to a fictitious town named for the national bird. And certainly not compared to the name of our state capital sixty miles away. With a bow to the French, Des Moines. Now there is a sexy name. We kids called it "Dez Mo Nez."

Greenfield. Nothing more than a simple description of what you should expect to see were you to go there for a visit in the summer: blankets of emerald-green grass.

Is my hometown memorable in any sense of the word? I will tell you the one remarkable trait of this town named after a patch of grass: It still has a magnetic pull on someone who has lived away from it for multiples of the number of years he lived in it. I have known many towns since then—lived in some big cities, lived in some suburbs—but none hold the force this little town still does all these years later. Like a robin returning in the springtime, I go back in my mind to the little town on the prairie to await those green fields of summer.

ADAIR COUNTY, STATE OF IOWA

"During the Civil War, the people were content with the idea of Fontanelle as the county seat, but at the end of the war it was brought to a vote. Changing the seat was defeated by seven votes. Again in 1869 the change was defeated. Finally, in 1874, voters approved the move to Greenfield. The decision was challenged and taken to the Supreme Court. Even though the decision wasn't final, the people of Greenfield moved the county records to their town. More than 200 men and 75 wagons made the trip to Fontanelle and, against the orders of the sheriff, loaded the records and furniture into their wagons and returned to Greenfield. It surprised Fontanelle's townspeople so much, they didn't resist."

From "About Adair County" on www.adaircountyiowa.org

I come from a family of truck drivers. Not long after Dad came home from WWII, he started driving for the G & H Motor Freight Lines, a short-haul outfit in his hometown of Greenfield. Thirty-some years and who knows how many miles later, he retired from G & H. Dad's brother drove a truck at one time, as did my brother and any number of cousins on the Porter side.

I didn't follow in the footsteps of my teamster kin. I studied to become an accountant, and in that respect I took after Mom. Up until the day she died, Mom "kept the books" for G & H Freight. I recall sitting at her desk, surrounded by stacks of invoices and bills of lading, mesmerized by the big ten-key Friden adding machine. Here I was in my element, not behind the wheel of a big rig.

Not that I didn't like riding in Dad's truck. Occasionally I would tag along with him to Des Moines to pick up freight. He would load freight at the warehouses in the capital city and then "peddle" it to the various merchants around Greenfield and the surrounding small towns the next day. On the way to Des Moines we would stop for coffee—chocolate milk for me, coffee for Dad—and a Bismarck at a tiny diner in Winterset. From there it was on to Des Moines by way of the two-lane highways, Ike's interstate system still a few years away.

There was a favorite game we often played as we bounced along in the truck. The entire premise was based on the fact that in those days Iowa's license plates didn't have the names of the counties on them. Instead, each county was assigned a number, that number corresponding to the county's place alphabetically among Iowa's 99 counties. I took no small amount of pride in the fact that Greenfield was the seat of ADAIR County, the number-one county in the entire state. Sorry ADAMS County, which happened to be next door to us. You may start off with "ADA," but an "I" trumps an "M" every time.

Our game boiled down to me trying to stump Dad. I would catch a glimpse at the license plate on a car approaching from the opposite direction and call out the number to him. His challenge was to see how quickly he could rattle off the name of the county.

That was a 52, I would call out from my perch in the passenger's seat.

Johnson County, he would holler over the roar of the truck's engine.

Number 77.

Way too easy. Everyone knows that is Polk, Dad would quickly reply, taking a puff from his ever-present pipe.

There goes a 31, I would call, thinking for certain I would be able to stump him.

That would be Dubuque County. Need to get up pretty early, sonny, to get one past me, he would proudly proclaim after just the slightest hesitation on a county from the opposite corner of the state. Our game went on until we reached Des Moines.

It must be the bean-counter in me. There is something special about a state with 99 counties. Not 98 and not 100, but 99. No other state in the Union has 99. Big old Texas has 254, way too many. Tiny Delaware has but three, so I say why bother? Yes sir, something extra special about a state with 99 counties.

There's something even more special about hailing from the number-one county in that state. And being able to claim no less than three relatives who served the number-one county in various capacities. It began with Grandpa Porter, the sheriff of Adair County from 1914-1916 (a man of multiple talents, he also had stints as a barber and as the manager of the liquor store). One of his sons, my Uncle Max, was the clerk of court for many years. Closer to home, my mother served as the secretary of the Adair County Fair, right up until the time of her death.

Greenfield wasn't always the county seat. Fontanelle, which is five miles to the west, originally housed the county courthouse. After a few years of nasty tug of war, those renegades from Greenfield eventually packed up the county records one last time and moved them five miles east. They reside there to this day, in the old courthouse anchoring the center of the town square.

I sympathize with Fontanelle, but I am glad my hometown persevered. Only a select few can say they grew up in a county seat that is the *first* in a state with 99 counties. Greenfield, Adair County, State of Iowa.

SATURDAY ON
THE TOWN SQUARE

*"Town Night on the square offered a variety of businesses
to frequent, a movie to see, a good meal at a small town café,
and a snow cone or popcorn from Eddie's Super Popcorn Stand."*

From "History" on www.greenfieldiowa.com

Fifty years later, no need for a GPS. I just close my eyes and I'm
back on the old town square…

Up the alley to peek in the window of the pool hall. Old men
in bib overalls hunch over a snooker table, their leathery chins
dripping tobacco juice. I can taste a mellow Mountain Dew from
the pop machine, but I resist the temptation to step inside. My
mother's edict: The pool hall is off-limits to a kid of thirteen. Not
because they sell liquor—they don't, though I often wonder why
the old men occasionally disappear into the back room. It's the
language, even stronger than the fragrance of fresh manure on
the farmers' boots.

The square is beginning to fill with pickups, each sporting
a thick layer of dust like frosting on a cake, compliments of the
gravel washboards the farmers drive to town. It's a Saturday, the
day they come to town to shop. Any "official" business will have to
wait for another day. That takes place at the county courthouse in

the middle of the square. Weekdays, Uncle Max would welcome me in to explore his massive steel vault. The dusty, leather-bound books there tell the history of our county as it pertains to the good, the bad, and the ugly—marriages, births, deaths, and divorces.

I stop to gaze in the window display at Crooks Clothing. The new Converse high tops have arrived, the shoes that will earn me my first letter. The letter I'll proudly wear on one of those shiny black-and-gold jackets hanging in the window.

I glance up at the marquee above the Grand Theatre to see what's playing this Saturday night. A blob engulfing an entire town? Elvis strumming a guitar at a Hawaiian luau? Or Moses parting the Red Sea? I'll surely be back tonight, but now I have to hurry along. Can't be late for my first day at the grocery store. I reach in my pocket for my clip-on tie. Along with the short-sleeved white shirt and black slacks, they make up the uniform of an official stock shelfer and bag sacker. So far, my jobs have been of the neighborhood variety—shoveling walks, mowing lawns, delivering newspapers. This is a major step up, 90 cents an hour and a clip-on tie.

If I had more time, I'd stop in the Carnegie. Who knows what waits for me there? I might hear the howling of a wolf on the Yukon, ride along with Huck and Jim down the Mississippi, or even help fight the Germans on the Rhine.

Now I've just enough time to peep through the smoke-stained glass of the beer joint in back of the grocery store. A townie gives me a smug look as he hustles out with a six pack under his arm, lighting a Camel with his free hand. My senses come alive as I gaze inside. The bright blue neon of the jovial Hamm's bear logo lit up over the bar. The cold, crisp taste—or so I suspect—of a frothy draft from the land of sky-blue waters. Warm, salted beer nuts in a jar on the counter. And as the screen door opens for another early-morning disciple, the sweet melody of "I Want to Hold Your Hand" by the Beatles on the jukebox.

I hustle into the grocery store, treated to the aroma of fresh fruit and apple fritters. I clip on my tie, put on an apron, and begin a Saturday on the town square.

This essay appeared in the *River Falls Journal* on February 23, 2012.

ODE TO A SWIMMING POOL

Like a 60-Year-Old Lady

*"In this age of giant water slides, artificial wave machines
and simulated roaring rivers, the Greenfield Municipal
Swimming Pool with its three diving boards stands
out like a 60-year-old lady in a mini-skirted crowd."*

From Ed Sidey's column in the *Adair County Free Press*, July 3, 2002

To the Greenfield Swimming Pool,

Happy birthday, old friend! I heard that you turned sixty.
Although that would make you eight years older than me, I feel
like we grew up together. I was the scrawny little kid who lived
across the street from you. To my brother and me, you were synonymous with summer—one and the same. This was a time before
video games and soccer camps, when summers meant spending
the days running back and forth across the street to visit you. If we
weren't taking a dip in your cooling waters, we were engaged in a
hotly contested game of baseball on your finely manicured lawn.

While we kept a watchful eye on you from the north, our
cousins the Martins held the same kind of lookout post from the
west. And they served you well as lifeguards. First it was Jacque,
the oldest of them, and next was Pam, my classmate. Even before

them, our cousins on the other side of the family, Ranny and Pat, worked for you. I always thought the cousins cut us a bit of slack since we were, after all, cousins.

You used to shine your lights in my bedroom window, but I didn't mind. These were those extra-special nights when someone rented you for an after-hours party. If we really wanted to know what was going on over there without being invited, we would just camp out on our front porch with a panoramic view of the festivities across the street. Usually by about eleven o'clock the party would come to a close. If you listened carefully, you could even hear the big switch that someone threw to turn off the lights.

George Whitworth, Pat Ray, and Ken Sanders. These were my heroes growing up with you. George, the manager, was the ultimate authority figure; but if he liked you, he saw that you got treated pretty well. I can still hear him humming along to the latest tunes belting away on KIOA radio. And while George represented authority, lifeguards Pat and Ken were the epitome of what we young kids wanted to grow up to be. About the first of August they would start lobbing a football around on the grass that separated you from our yard. They may just as well have been Bart Starr and Paul Hornung—that's how larger-than-life they seemed to me.

The biggest contest of the year revolved around opening day. Who would be the very first in line and thus the first to enter your bathhouse for the year? Who would be the first to actually get in the water? And who the first off each diving board? All these were highly coveted honors that could distinguish a young swimmer for the entire season.

Oh, your diving boards always presented a challenge. How many different ways could we find to make a good impression on anyone watching and still not crack our skulls wide open in the process? That was the dilemma on the massive, unforgiving block of white concrete with red lettering we all knew as the "high dive." How about a back flip? No. Maybe a gainer would set the crowd on its feet? Or maybe, just for the challenge, a cannonball off one of the sideboards to see how many unsuspecting sunbathers stretched out on nice, dry beach towels we could soak.

And what was the all-time record for the shortest time in the water before getting kicked out by one of the lifeguards? Heck, sometimes you didn't even make it to the water—you might get an early shower just for running on the concrete, something everyone knew was a cardinal sin. Another way to exit before you entered was if the lifeguards realized you had not taken the obligatory shower with soap before putting your suit on—now, how could they possibly have known this?

Another regular contest for my buddies and me was seeing how many times we could visit you in a single day. I forget now what the record was for this feat, but whatever it was the sight of us coming and going all day certainly was enough to irritate the poor lifeguards.

A different sort of challenge arose when a kid had a few coins in his pocket. What type of candy should he buy? There were many choices, but it was always hard to resist a Slo Poke since you could buy it on one trip out of the pool and still be working on it on your return later in the day. You just didn't want to let any of the lifeguards catch you with food or drink when you crossed that magical line.

Even when you closed your doors for the summer, you still remained a part of our lives. Fall meant Pee Wee football, and

I vividly recall putting on our battle gear in your locker room. It was fascinating to see the bathhouse in an entirely different light. By this time, you were completely winterized and the sights and sounds of the summer were just a fading memory. I can still hear our volunteer coach "Monk" Wright firing up the squad as we left your dressing room for another battle with the Guthrie Center Pee Wees.

Chlorine in my eyes—none of us thought of wearing goggles back then. Chills up and down my arms as I hustled home with a towel wrapped around me on days when it was so cold the lifeguards didn't want to be there—but a few of us showed up anyway. And the skin on my toes wrinkled from so many visits to you on a single day—but I still couldn't break the one-day record. Thanks for helping me recall some wonderful memories that could only come from growing up next to you.

And happy No. 60!

This essay appeared in the *Adair County Free Press* on July 3, 2002.

PICTURES

"The staff of the Greenfield swimming pool has been kept plenty busy so far this season, as the pool enjoyed its biggest opening week in many years. Left to right are, front row, attendants Carole Cunningham, Linda Butler, Jean Musmaker and Cynthia Welcher; back row, Pat Ray, assistant manager, Linda Bergmann, life guard and George Whitworth, manager."

From the *Adair County Free Press*, June 19, 1963

Every picture tells a story. Stories of life, stories of death; some of happy times, others of sad times. This picture tells many stories. The first is a story of life, and from the looks on the faces of the lifeguards, of happy times. This snapshot captures the Greenfield Swimming Pool staff in 1963, posing for what seems to be the official photo run in the *Adair County Free Press* to herald the start of another season of splishing and splashing.

Four young girls in one-piece bathing suits stand in the front row—two with hands clasped in front of them, the other two with hands dangling at their sides. The back row is reserved for a taller girl, flanked on each side by two guys, each shirtless. The boy on the left is all-American, every bit a young Robert Redford. On the right is the pool manager, a few years older than the others, wearing glasses and a look of confidence fitting for someone in charge.

The picture is black and white, but not in my mind. I see a kaleidoscope of colors. I see bright stripes on the suit of one of the lifeguards in the front row, a colorful floral design on the petite girl next to her. The pool behind glistens an aqua blue.

KIOA FM, Des Moines, Iowa, plays on the radio in the bathhouse in front of the lifeguards. Gary Lewis and the Playboys advise that it's okay to have a summer fling or two, but to save your heart for me. Chad and Jeremy sing of trees swayin' in the summer breeze, but remind us that all good things must end someday. The large, leafy tree behind the lifeguards does just that, sways in the summer breeze.

The expansive lawn in the background of the picture is not black and white, but a brilliant emerald green, as it should be on a gorgeous June day in Iowa. That was our playground, the site of pickup baseball and football. The lawn could tell its own stories—of the jarring hits it took from young lads flinging each other to the ground in games of "touch" football, of bats slammed to its surface on a "no way was that over the plate" called third strike.

But the lawn never protested. It was content to be included in the action, only needing a good soaking rain every so often to keep its luster. Yes, Chad and Jeremy, all good things must end someday. Autumn leaves will certainly fall. The lawn's coat will fade in the dog days of summer, the August sun turning the green grass to a parched brown. But for now, all is right with the world.

This picture has other stories to tell, some that took place across the street on the north side of Dodge Street. Look in the background of the picture. Perfectly framed between the heads of the young Redford and the lanky girl in the back row is a two-story house. That two-story house was the only home I knew for the first eighteen years of my life, up until the day I left for college.

Two other houses are visible in the picture. The one to the right, the Beaman house. The one to the left, the Umbaugh house. Back then, in more stable times, houses were identified by the occupants. The Beaman house, the Umbaugh house. The second house to the left of ours, not in the picture, is Pete Funke's house. Pete worked for the county, driving the maintainer that smoothed out its gravel roads. His front porch was the perch from which the two of us spent summer evenings solving the problems of the world and spitting watermelon seeds.

Two windows are prominent in our house, one on the first floor and a smaller one on the second. The downstairs one was a "picture" window. These were common in the houses of that era—a large, rectangular window in a family's living room. Looking out, you had a view of the larger world outside. From the outside looking in, you could see the life of a family unfold in front of you —a life naturally lived in its living room.

The living room wasn't just for living though. It also served a morbid function. It was not unusual in the first part of the twentieth century to display the bodies of deceased loved ones in the living room prior to their internment. I was told our living room was where Grandpa Porter lay after he died in 1949, the year before I was born. So through that picture window, a passerby that year might have seen a casket displayed in our living room, at least for a few days. A year later that same passerby would have seen me laying in a crib in that same living room, now transformed from a room for the dead to one for the living. A resurrection of sorts.

Look through the picture window and you will see another picture. At least, I see it in my mind. It's a large Zenith console television. A Zenith was more than a TV; it was a piece of furniture. Our black-and-white TV occupied a spot on the north side of the living room, directly across from the picture window. Saturday nights, this is where Marshall Dillon came riding into our living room, Mom providing the refreshments of freshly popped corn served in silver metal bowls. Sunday nights, Ed Sullivan told us he had a really big show planned, complete with a kissing mouse named Topo Gigio.

Not all pictures on our Zenith were pleasant ones. Fast forward nearly five months to the day when the swimming pool staff appeared in the *Free Press*. On November 22, 1963, I was sent home from the eighth grade along with all the others at Greenfield Junior High. The soap opera, *As the World Turns*, stopped turning long enough for Walter Cronkite to break in with shocking news. He removed his large black glasses and glanced up at a clock on the wall. Then he turned to the camera and told America that, at 1:00 p.m. Central Time, the president was dead. For a brief, shining moment, there was Camelot. Now there was despair.

Along with the rest of the country, we watched the pictures on our Zenith over the next few days. Oath of office on an airplane. Gunshots in a crowded hallway. Salutes from a little boy in shorts. More gunshots, but these to memorialize the fallen leader.

It didn't take long for the nation's grief to be replaced with glee. Barely two months after the assassination—February 9, 1964— Ed Sullivan introduced the four young lads from Liverpool with five simple words: "Ladies and gentlemen, The Beatles." "All My Loving" told us we weren't alone, that there were better days ahead.

Pictures often fade in the light of day. Surprisingly, this picture—granted it is a black and white—is as clear as the day it was taken. Two generations later, are all seven lifeguards still living? I don't know, nor do I want to find out, easy as that would be in our wired world. For a brief, shining moment, the five young girls, the handsome kid with the crew cut, and the pool manager were royalty.

Living in Camelot.

Courtesy of The Sidey Collection®

ST. JOHN'S

"St. John's Catholic Church, complete with pews and stained glass windows, was dedicated September 7, 1907, fifty years ago. It was a great day, the sky was clear, the roads bad, the Church was blessed by Fathers Nugent, Bede and Alban; the Church was filled with Catholic and non-Catholic; High Mass was said by Father Bede Durham, O.S.B. [sic] beautiful music by St. Malachy's choir of Creston rang from the choir loft; September sunshine filtered through the stained glass windows."

From the souvenir booklet, dated November 10, 1957,
to commemorate the Golden Jubilee of St. John's Church, Greenfield, Iowa

The rhythmic sounds of *et in Spiritum Sanctum, Kyrie eleison, gloria in excelsis*. The pungent smell of burning incense. The chalky taste of communion wafers. The creepy feel of the crusty feet of the old men. The pleasing sight of a brilliant ruby-red cassock.

No other memories from my childhood stoke the sensory images as much as that institution around the corner from our house, across the street from the swimming pool. I speak of it as an institution, as there was so much more to it than just the edifice that housed St. John's Catholic Church.

My mother was a staunch Catholic, and a devout one at that. My father was the son of Methodist parents. But there was never any discussion I can recall as to where we boys would receive our spiritual education. Looking back, there must have been an explicit understanding between my parents that the boys would genuflect, take communion, observe the holy days, and practice all the habits that separated Catholics from the followers of John Wesley, Martin Luther, and John Calvin.

The Methodists, the Lutherans, the Presbyterians—these were the Protestants in town. We were different. We were the ones with ashes on our foreheads at the start of Lent. We were the ones eating cheese sandwiches on the bus after Friday night football games while the Protestants enjoyed their roast beef. We weren't vegetarians. No one was back then. It was just that Catholics abstained from meat on Fridays.

With a peculiar exception, I have no memory of ever setting foot in my dad's old Methodist church. Ironically, I spent the entire second grade in the basement of that church. A new elementary was under construction that year; we second graders were shuffled to the basement of the church to await our move the following year to the brand-new grade school on the north end of town.

I never thought of myself as anything other than Catholic. And Irish Catholic at that. Mom's ancestors, the Fagans, came over from County Queens in Ireland. Even though I carried the name Porter, I was always proud of my Irish heritage. There were also Eagans on Mom's side of the family. There's something lyrical about having Fagan and Eagan on the same side of the family tree. Equally lyrical was the name of one of Mom's uncles, Cornelius Eagan. What an unusual a name, Cornelius—Uncle Connie for short. The Fagans and the Eagans became linked when Helen "Nellie" Mae Fagan, my mother's namesake, married Connie Eagan.

Yes, there are so many sensory images from St. John's that remain with me to this day, a lifetime later. Many of them revolve around my duties as an altar boy (no thought of altar girls back then). We learned a dead language, not for purposes of conversing or writing in Latin, but for one of the altar boy's main tasks, reciting the prayers. *Benedictus Deus.* Maybe dead, but so exotic and mysterious to a young elementary school kid. A language kept on life support by us Catholics on the north side of town.

Our parish priest was Father Bartholomew Kane. Fittingly, he and I arrived in Greenfield the same year, 1950. Thirty-six years my senior, Father Kane came to St. John's in July from a parish of the same name in Des Moines. I came to St. John's for my baptism in September 1950, direct from the brand-new hospital on the east side of Greenfield. From that first introduction, Father Kane—the kind-hearted, soft-spoken Irishman—was my spiritual leader and one of the finest teachers I ever had.

Altar boys "served" Mass on a rotating basis, assigned weekday Mass every few weeks. It was early, but it wasn't as if you needed to be awake for weekday 7:00 a.m. Mass. Given how close our house was to St. John's, I suspect we were tabbed more often than some of the other boys in town. We could roll out of bed, put on a pair of jeans and a t-shirt, cut across the swimming pool lawn, and be in the sacristy within minutes, still half asleep.

The sacristy was a small room off to the side of the altar where we dressed for Mass, like ballplayers putting on their uniforms in the clubhouse. Instead of pinstripes, our standard garb consisted of a white surplus pulled over a black cassock, the brilliant red cassock reserved for holy days.

Holy days. Those mysterious days forever stamped in my memory. Some were solemn, like Holy Thursday and Good Friday; others were joyous, like Easter Sunday and Christmas Eve. Holy Week itself was filled with every conceivable form of symbolism known to mankind. It started with Palm Sunday. This was the one time we Catholics took our show on the road, marching ceremoniously a few blocks up and down Elm Street while carrying our palms. Father Kane instructed us in the fine art of weaving palms to make all sorts of ingenuous designs.

Next came Holy Thursday and the Last Supper. Twelve of the oldest men in the parish came forward to have their feet washed, symbolic of what took place at the original Last Supper. As altar boys we had a very specific task assigned to us: We held out the towel for Father Kane to use after he dipped the calloused, crusty feet of the old men in the basins.

The next day, Holy Friday, was the most solemn of them all. Black. The only color visible on the altar during the afternoon's service. Even the fourteen stations of the cross along the walls of the church were draped in black. Black was also the color of the substance giving off the strong scent on Good Friday. Incense. It travelled straight up your nose as you kneeled with the "boat," the censer directly below you. At the appropriate time, you passed the censer to the priest, who then began waving it out in front of him, chanting Latin prayers as he went along. Another unforgettable memory from that day is a visual one: a picture of the priest lying facedown on the floor of the altar. Facedown, praying. After what seemed an eternity, the priest would eventually pick himself up off the floor and continue the service.

Easter Sunday was the antithesis. Now we were decked out in the brilliant red cassocks and celebrated the wonder of the day before heading home to feast. In the early years, we would have started the day at home with the traditional Easter egg hunt.

Eventually, Father Kane moved on. By the time I got to high school, Father Kane became Monsignor Kane, and with the new title came a promotion to a larger parish. Not that much different than any other servant, whether working for the man or working for The Man. You do a good job, and you move up the ladder. In this instance, the ladder leading to heaven. He may have assumed a new title, but Monsignor Kane would always just be Father Kane to me.

"They" came around once a year in the spring and stayed for a week. It was the only time of the year we saw any religious sort in anything other than priest's garb. "They" were the nuns. The Benedictine Sisters. The penguins, if you subscribe to the sort of religious beliefs of Jake and Elwood in *The Blues Brothers*. However, I don't recall ever receiving any sort of serious rebuke from our nuns, unlike the infamous brothers. Our sisters were there to teach us history, specifically the history of the Bible. That history was neatly packaged into a little blue paperback book covering the two distinct periods: B.C. and A.D. For no particular reason, I had a preference for the B.C. history. I found something thrilling about starting at the very beginning with Adam and Eve, moving on to Abraham, and following Moses up the mountainside.

After Father Kane moved up the hierarchy in the Catholic Church, we had a new priest in town. You could say a new sheriff in town, the replacement being more the disciplinarian, as opposed to Father Kane the teacher. One particular episode will illustrate my point.

My buddy, Gary Keese, and I were holed up in the choir loft one Sunday morning, figuring this was the best place to carry on a conversation that would go unnoticed down below amongst the devout parishioners. A chance for us to debate the relative merits of Sandy Koufax versus Juan Marichal as the starting pitcher for the National League in the All-Star Game. All was going well until the priest glanced up to the choir loft. In short order, he directed us to shut up. Paraphrasing all these years later, it was to the effect of, *Keese and Porter, this is the liturgy of the Eucharist. You shall be quiet and pay attention.* You could have heard the proverbial pin drop, made all the easier by the terrazzo floors in the old church.

Needless to say, I got an earful from my mother as we crossed the swimming pool yard on the short walk home that day. I am thankful to this day that the walk was as short as it was. Much to my chagrin, I found out later that my buddy got off scot-free from his mom. He convinced her there was no calling out of "Keese and Porter" in the choir loft. No, it was just the beginning of a prayer, "Peace and Order." Showing these early signs of a way with words, it was no surprise to any of us kids that Gary Keese eventually became a lawyer.

St. John's is long gone. I don't mean to imply there is no longer a Catholic parish in Greenfield. There is, a very vibrant one at that. What is gone is the old church itself, torn down and replaced by a more contemporary-looking building in 1972, the year I graduated college and moved out of state.

In my memory, St. John's will always be that old rectangular edifice with the terrazzo floors and the bell in the tower that rang out to remind a young boy it was time to hustle across the swimming pool yard, put on a cassock, and serve Mass.

Vade in pacem.

SUNDAY DINNER

*"Every Cut of Proten [sic] Beef Guaranteed Tender
Every Time. Boneless Rolled Yankee Pot Roast...LB. 49c."*

From a Berg's Sure Save Market ad appearing
in the *Adair County Free Press*, July 1, 1964

The only time we ate dinner at our house was on Sundays. I shouldn't give the impression that we ate out every other day of the week, preposterous as that would have been in a small Iowa town in the fifties. It's just that this time period and setting had its own nomenclature. "Dinner" was the noon meal on Sundays. "Lunch" was the noon meal and "supper" the evening meal all other days of the week. "Brunch" was not part of our vocabulary. It didn't matter what day of the week it was, we had breakfast every morning. Early. So we didn't combine breakfast on Sundays with the noonday dinner. And if we did, wouldn't it have been "brinner" rather than "brunch"? Finally, Sunday evening supper had its very own name: leftovers.

Mom had an incredible knack for effortlessly—or so it seemed to me—preparing Sunday dinner. She started early, before we left the house to walk the one block over to St. John's for Mass. Before crock pots and microwaves, a roast was placed in the oven, slowly simmering as we gave glory to God and prayed in Latin with

Father Kane. As we cut across the swimming pool lawn on our way home after Mass, I could already smell the roast, its aroma filtering through the screen door—a door that was only locked if we were going to be gone overnight.

Once we were back home, Mom swung into full gear, boiling the potatoes, shelling the garden-fresh peas, and sifting off the grease from the roast to make gravy. A multi-tasker before that term was ever invented, she would grab the ancient rolling pin that had been in the family for years and begin rolling out the dough for one of her famous pies. As was the case with all her dishes, there was no recipe, no *Joy of Cooking* or celebrity television show to consult on how to make that perfect cherry pie. If anyone asked her what went in the pies—as my wife, Melissa, did when she first visited our home—she answered in her honest, no-nonsense way: *Oh, a little of this and a little of that.*

Cherry pie was always my favorite, probably because the cherries came from an old tree directly out the kitchen window. And having had a literal hand in the final product—picking the ripe, red cherries from that tree—must have something to do with my preference to this day for cherry pies over all other kinds. Mom showed horses, not food; but if she had, her blueberry, peach, and apple pies would have been blue ribbons and her cherry pie the Grand Champion.

Back to Sundays. At five to noon, Mom would announce, *Dinner is on the table.* Her voice carried to the living room, two rooms removed from the kitchen. The living room was where the menfolk would be positioned in front of the black-and-white Zenith, watching the Bears and the Packers from Soldier Field in Chicago, staying out of Mom's way. Our dining room separated the kitchen from the living room, but it was reserved for special Sunday dinners, such as Thanksgiving, Christmas, and Easter. Most Sundays we ate dinner in the kitchen.

The announcement came at five minutes before the hour to ensure we would all be seated and ready to dig in at noon, straight up. This was when we ate dinner, or lunch during the week, just as 6:00 was the appointed time for supper. Not 12:30, not 1:00, but at precisely noon. I have never really been able to offer a logical explanation for the need to eat dinner at exactly noon. Rarely did we have any pressing commitments on Sunday afternoons other than letting our bellies rest from the feast Mom put on the table. It was simply in our DNA that noon and 6:00 were when you ate your meals.

To this day I can still taste Sunday dinner. Roast beef so tender you could cut it with your fork. Real mashed potatoes, with enough cholesterol in the guise of milk and butter to send your ratio over the top (not that we had a clue what that was back then). Sweet peas fresh from the garden. And that delicacy of all delicacies: cherry pie with a dollop of homemade ice cream on top. No mistaking, this was not lunch, brunch, or supper. This was Sunday dinner at our house.

Courtesy of The Sidey Collection®

AUNT GRACIE AND UNCLE AB

"I was a young lad when a portion of the sanitary sewer for Greenfield was built. For most of a summer, I stood in our front yard while Albert Foster dug the sewer line in front of our house. He did a good job. The ditch he dug was deep and very straight."

From Ed Sidey's column in the
Adair County Free Press, October 25, 2006

We lived on the north edge of town. If you walked to the west end of our block and then straight south to the other end of town, you would be at their place. Their place consisted of a small, white, one-story, wood-frame house with a few outbuildings, a garden they tended, and a pasture where they raised a few head of livestock. Grace and Albert Foster were really my *great* aunt and uncle. A young boy like me wouldn't have given it much thought at the time, but there was probably a logical reason why I so gravitated to the two of them. Grace's brother, John, was my grandfather, but he died before I was born. Albert was like a grandfather, with Gracie as a second grandmother thrown in for good measure.

These two gentle folks have now been gone for decades, and the passage of that much time causes the memory to fade some. But certain details about them and their life are as clear in my mind as if it were yesterday. As if yesterday were a lazy summer afternoon and our family was pulling into their gravel drive in our pink '57 Pontiac for a Sunday picnic of fried chicken, mashed potatoes, and vegetables fresh from the garden.

The senses immediately came alive, but not just those of the aromatic variety. For starters, there was the blare from the television set. Albert's hearing had begun to fail him. His solution to the practical issue of making sure he could hear the latest episode of one of his favorite westerns was to crank the volume as far to the right as it would go. Marshall Dillon's voice was crystal clear from the backseat of our car as we pulled in the driveway.

Once Aunt Grace could get Uncle Albert's attention to let him know company had arrived, they would both be in the front yard to greet us. The two of them were little people. Not in heart, but in outward appearance. Their diminutive size seemed typical of a generation born well before the start of the twentieth century and given to a life of hard physical labor.

That Grace and Albert were no strangers to strenuous work was evident in their standard dress. Albert wore bib overalls with a fresh shirt for Sunday dinner. (Yes, he wears a suit in the picture included here, but the occasion was their sixtieth wedding anniversary.) Grace would shuffle out the door in her housedress and tennis shoes, broom in hand. Her tennis shoes were never intended as a fashion statement. They weren't Nikes. Her simple canvas shoes were cut out in the front to allow room for her bunion.

Albert always had his signature cigar dangling from the side of his mouth. Not to worry, Surgeon General. Albert didn't smoke his cigars. He chewed them. My theory on this habit had to do with another of his physical ailments. In addition to trouble hearing in his later years, Albert's hands were given to extreme shaking, making it very challenging to strike a match and keep a cigar lit. Thus, his penchant to chew them and the need for the spittoon in the front room next to the blaring TV.

Gracie and Ab—as they were fondly called by those who adored them—were legendary for their generosity, which was not in the slightest way due to any material wealth. They lived a simple life and believed in sharing what they had with others. A few examples illustrate the point.

It was not unusual for our family to have an entire side of beef in our stand-up freezer in the kitchen. Although I was too young to know much about family finances, it was common knowledge that when Ab sent a steer to the butcher, Mom and Dad paid far below market price to fill that freezer. In addition to raising a few cattle, Ab mowed yards for some of the elderly widows in town, again at heavily discounted rates. I'm guessing he dug that sewer line Ed Sidey recalls at far less than anyone else would have charged. And when it came time for us to leave those family picnics, he would follow us kids out to the car, frantically trying to stuff quarters and half dollars into our pockets. At the same time, Gracie could be heard from her kitchen urging us to "take home a little loaf of bread." Her freshly baked bread, spread with real butter, was right up there among the true pleasures in life with homemade ice cream and fresh sweet corn from the garden.

Dad developed a habit over the years of saving funeral cards— obituaries, if you will. Now that he and most of his generation are gone, I consider them a prized possession, a link to the past. As I look back at Grace and Albert's obituaries, a few of the details stick out. Albert lived to be almost ninety years old, Grace eighty-six. And, after a life of about seventy years together, they died barely a year apart—Albert in 1969 and Grace the following year. Both "passed on at the Greenfield Rest Home," a place that at the time would have been referred to as an "old-folks home." Fitting indeed that these dear old folks would spend their final days on this earth resting together.

Rest well, Gracie and Ab. You deserve it.

Personal Collection

PETE

"The Adair County Engineer is responsible for the construction and maintenance of the Secondary Road System of Adair County, Iowa. The road system is made up of approximately 1016 miles of roads; 793 gravel, 135 earth and 88 miles paved."

From adaircountyiowa.org

Pete Funke drove a maintainer for the county. A maintainer is essentially a giant tractor with a blade the width of a small house underneath it to smooth out gravel roads. In rural Iowa in the fifties, maintaining the gravel roads was a high priority. Without it, navigating one of the many rocky roads was like driving on a washboard. Pete's daily grind was crucial to the well-being of the citizens of Adair County.

Pete was our neighbor two houses down, on the corner of our block. His daughter, Louise, was our babysitter when Mom bucked the trend at that time and took a job "outside the home." Too young to enunciate "Louise" properly, she became "Weezie" and remains so to this day, some sixty years later.

Two images of Pete. First, the only place I can picture him is on his front porch. I can't recall ever seeing him around town. Given the nature of his bone-jarring work, once home he seemed content to stay there and just kick back. The second image is his attire. I never saw Pete in anything other than his overalls, standard dress in the day for not only farmers but anyone performing manual labor. Tucked into one of the front pockets of his bibs was his pipe and a pouch of Prince Albert.

Pete and I visited on his front porch. Back in the fifties, that's what neighbors in a small town did—they visited. Visiting seems to be a lost art. Done correctly, there is much more to it than meets the eye, much more than two people exchanging information. Done correctly, it is an art form. A pause, allowing time to reflect on something someone said, is as important as anything that *is* said. Any meaningful visiting also involves some reference to the weather—at least in the Midwest it does. *Sure is humid tonight. Quite a thunderstorm in the night, wasn't it? Heard they picked up two inches in Orient. Hail the size of golf balls.*

Sometimes Pete and I visited, and at other times we just sat and took in the soothing sounds of a warm summer's eve. Crickets chirping. Chatter from the Wright kids across the street playing in their drive way. The splash from a boy doing a cannonball over at the pool. Sometimes we indulged our taste buds as well. By mid-summer, the watermelons were ripe and the two of us would savor a slice, spitting the seeds off his porch onto the lawn.

Pete's front porch gave us a front-row seat as the action on the stage—that is, the people either walking or driving on the two streets easily visible from our vantage point—played out night after night during the summer. Teenage boys in their revved-up cars would cruise the block, working hard to impress some of the girls hanging out over at the pool. Flick a cigarette out the window. Peel some rubber. Crank up KIOA on the radio dial.

Not all the cars passing for our review were hot rods driven by the young bucks. Older folks would also be out, taking a leisurely drive around town. Invariably, at some point during the evening one of these cars would idle by, eliciting a response from Pete I can still recall.

You heard what happened to Joe, didn't you? Pete would say between long drags on his Prince-Albert-filled pipe.

Pete's utterance may have been in the form of a question, but it was no more a question than if I were to say, *Darn, that was some sweet melon we just ate!*

No, Pete. I don't think I heard about Joe, I would answer to Pete's delight, both of us noticing that Joe was sitting in the passenger's seat while the missus drove, not the usual arrangement in a small town.

This was just the response Pete was looking for, as it gave him the entrée needed to pass on the latest about poor old Joe. Maybe Joe was riding shotgun because he was recovering from some surgery. Maybe he had lost his license after his third DWI. Perhaps his eyes were failing him.

It really didn't matter why Joe wasn't driving. The important thing was that Pete and I were visiting and those parading by were fodder for our visits, just as fruitful as the latest weather report. And as long as the rain held off, Pete would be back the next morning, driving a maintainer for the county.

Courtesy of The Sidey Collection®

PEE WEE

Greenfield Pee Wees Complete Season

*"Greenfield's football Pee Wees, sponsored by the
local Lions Club, recently completed their season,
which included four games against Guthrie Center."*

From the *Adair County Free Press*, November 1, 1961

Young kids, town and country alike, pick up nicknames. Depending
on how you look at it, I was the "lucky" recipient of two tags
during my school days. One of these stuck. To this day, I will
hear someone call "Otis" when I'm walking the streets of home,
a nickname courtesy of my cousin, Jake Jacobson, during a lull
in a junior high class.

The other moniker was a nod to my diminutive stature: Pee
Wee. The name suited me perfectly when I suited up for the
Greenfield Pee Wee football team, on the swimming pool lawn
directly across the street from our house. Others on the team were
imposters, much too big to fit the name. Not me. I was a real-life
Pee Wee, even with shoulder pads. That's me in the left-hand corner
of the front row, number 20. Even though I was one of the oldest
on the team as a sixth grader, I was also one of the smallest. A
mimeographed roster from that year lists me at 67 pounds.

Some people know their birth weight, not because they stepped onto a scale out of the womb, but because it was recorded for posterity. The stat that will forever be emblazoned in my memory is one that came along my freshmen year of high school. Eighty. No, not my height in inches. I could only have dreamed to be 6-foot 8. At that verticality, I would have been the star on the Greenfield Tigers basketball team. Dunking, slamming, jamming, and leading the local five to four consecutive state titles at Vets Auditorium in Des Moines. But I wasn't 6-foot 8, and I didn't lead the team in scoring. No, the number 80 wasn't my height, but rather my weight—in pounds—in high school.

In those days, and at a small school such as ours, there was no soccer team, no cross country. Boys who wanted to be on a team in the fall went out for football. And there were no tryouts during which the slower, smaller kids (think Pee Wee) were mercilessly cut. The result was that so many boys went out for football there were not enough left to field a marching band. Too many budding halfbacks and linebackers and not enough trombonists and trumpeters.

Journalists are always looking for an angle and here was a tailor-made one. Small town school has a problem fielding a marching band. All the boys go out for football.

I will never forget the day. I was sitting in freshman algebra, trying to make what sense I could out of variables, coefficients, and constants. Coach appeared in the doorway of the classroom with a writer from the *Des Moines Tribune* in tow. Coach spotted me and with a simple movement of his index finger directed me to step outside in the hallway. When he directed you to do something, you didn't explain that you couldn't, that you were too busy trying to make sense out of variables, coefficients, and constants. No, when Coach summoned you, you sprung to attention.

Seems they wanted to get a picture of the little guy. How about that water fountain over there—the type most kids would need to lean down to use, not stand up on their tiptoes like Yours Truly. Let's snap a picture of Pee Wee stretching every inch of his scrawny frame to reach the H_2O.

So there it was. A feature story in the largest daily rag in the state of Iowa, telling how this small town had too many ballplayers and not enough musicians for a marching band. Plenty of flutists, not enough tubists. Enough majorettes, not enough majors. And to top it off, we have what we think may be the smallest player in the state, at 80 pounds dripping wet. Each of the stars on the team, mostly upperclassmen (the studs), had those little headshots in the article. Here was my picture at the water fountain, a shot that took up half the entire length of a page. I didn't know whether to be honored or humiliated. It could go either way, fragile as an ego can be for a high school freshman.

When you were a scrawny, 80-pound football player, the only action you were going to see was during the week on the practice squad. The practice squad served one purpose and one purpose only: to run the plays likely to be run in the next game by the opponent. We were actors on the forlorn patch of ground a few blocks south of the high school that served as our stage. Stunt men, if you will; but with my diminutive stature, more of a stunt boy.

We huddle a few yards behind the line of scrimmage, looking nervously up at the assistant coach holding a clipboard with the next play diagrammed for us. I pray, please don't call my number.

I will gladly block or fake a reverse left. I promise not to trip or fake an injury if you promise not to call my number. But sometimes our prayers aren't answered. Halfback off right tackle, on the count of three. Break the huddle, boys.

Across the line of scrimmage is the first-team defense. These studs never viewed this cruelty as men against boys, when in fact that is precisely what it was. Each of us was a Daniel, being thrown to the lions across the line of scrimmage. I look into the beady eyes of the gargantuan linemen, sweat dripping off their enormous biceps. They are all frothing at the mouth, predators ready to attack their prey.

I adjust the chin strap on my helmet, as one would tighten their seatbelt when getting ready for a thrill ride at the state fair. I use my tongue to push my mouth guard into position, wanting to keep all my pearly whites intact. Nervously, I reach down to make sure my jock strap is firmly in place—protecting the family jewels, being an adolescent still in the developing stages.

For what seems like an eternity, the practice squad quarterback barks out signals. Brave boy is he. He knows his only challenge is to hand the ball off to me before any of the oversized linemen can cross the line and flatten him. The ball is snapped; the QB pivots effortlessly and hands it off to me.

Before I can even reach the line of scrimmage, I spy an immovable force coming my way, one of the gargantuan first-team linemen. Any one of them outweighed me by 150 pounds, and they all had a job to do: pummeling undersized halfbacks into oblivion.

It is too late. Slow as I am, it is too late to retreat in the other direction. After all, my lack of speed is one of the main reasons I have been assigned to the practice squad in the first place. I have no choice but to slow up even more in the nanosecond it takes the first-teamer to lower his head into my abdomen.

Most of us have gaps in our memory. The gap in my memory in this instance was induced by the lineman's powerful hit. My next recollection is looking up to see Coach standing over me with an ammonia tablet, better known as smelling salts.

I survived, as all of us on that practice squad did. Our work for the week was over. Now we could rest up, find a good vantage point on the bench to watch the Friday night game, and try not to think about the following Wednesday when we would again be fodder.

Four years later, when I graduated, I had ballooned up to somewhere in the neighborhood of 120 pounds, a real hunk of a man. But still Pee Wee to my classmates.

Courtesy of The Sidey Collection®

COACH

**Tigers Will Open Football
Season Here Against Creston Friday**

*"Here is the squad that will be carrying Greenfield High School
hopes for another winning football season this fall. The Tigers open
here this Friday evening at 7:30 against traditional foe Creston."*

From the *Adair County Free Press*, September 9, 1964

That's me in the second row, far right—same number 20 as I wore
on the Pee Wee team, now in my freshman year of high school.
Looking back, it seems fitting I would be kneeling just under the
watchful gaze of Coach in the last row. To add the last name was
unnecessary, and to call him by his first name, Lonnie…well, that
was unthinkable. To me, he was—and always will be—just "Coach."

Coach came to town in 1961, and by the next year he was my
junior high science teacher. He had been a college football player
and wrestler, tipping the scales I would guess at about 220, amply
filling out his 6-foot frame.

Coach sported a crew cut, a reflection of his no-nonsense
approach to life in general, and to teaching students in particular.
He always wore a crisp, highly starched, short-sleeved white shirt
with a tie. Freshly pressed slacks and wing-tips that shone so

bright you could see your reflection rounded out his attire. As was fashionable in the day, many of his shirts had his initials, LDT, monogrammed above the pocket.

Suffice it to say student conduct was never an issue in Coach's classes. His mere physical presence was enough to keep even the boldest student in line. Looking back, it seems fitting that Coach taught science. For him, there were no gray areas of uncertainty in life. For us, his students, the classroom was a laboratory in living.

Coach and I crossed paths again as soon as I walked out the door of the junior high building and down the sidewalk to the high school. He was the head football coach for the Greenfield Tigers, and he urged me to consider coming out for the team. At the time it seemed hard to understand why any coach would want me. Small as I was, I wasn't likely to strike any fear into the opposing players' hearts.

But Coach was a master motivator, and he saw my role on the team as the TSHCI: Third-String Halfback in Charge of Inspiration. Needless to say, I didn't see much playing time on Friday nights, even by the time I had swelled to a whopping 120 pounds my senior year. My mother was perfectly content to look down from the stands and see me firmly ensconced on the bench. On those rare occasions when I did get in at the end of a blowout, she was a nervous wreck.

I only recall one time when I incurred the wrath of Coach. At the time of the incident, all Coach had to say was that he was "disappointed" in me and my buddy, Curt Weber. I took this as a sure sign that his overall evaluation of my character was a good one. Logic says that when you commit a transgression, better that your superior be *disappointed* in you than *expecting* it from you.

The incident happened on the Friday afternoon of home-coming. After the parade on the square, all of us on the team were to return pronto to the school to shine our cleats, put on our game faces, and start focusing on that night's opponent. When the parade ended, Curt and I sensed a short window of opportunity for a quick game of eight ball before heading back to the school. One quick game turned into best two out of three, and before long we realized the error of our ways. When we arrived at the locker room, we came face to face with the man we had "disappointed."

The transgression resulted in a few extra laps around the track at the next week's practices. Never again did Coach have a reason to be disappointed in me. The lesson also made a favorable impression on my partner-in-crime. Curt Weber went on to have a long career in the classroom and in coaching—guess what—high school football.

Before the last of the autumn leaves had fallen from the trees in town, and sometime before the first snowflakes, my attention turned to my first love: the game of basketball. Coach's attention turned to his passion: his up-and-coming wrestling program. Given my diminutive size, he eyed me like a hungry dog would someone holding out a bone. With the lightest class at the time being 95 pounds, here was a kid who would never have to worry about making weight. Try as he might, and as much as I looked up to him, Coach could never convince me to give up my love for basketball. But my respect for him never waned, and each fall for the next two years I returned to the gridiron and strapped on my helmet for another season of practice squads during the week and bench-warming on Friday nights.

Even though he fielded some good football teams, it was Coach's success with the wrestling program that brought him the most press. And before long, his success landed him a chance to go to the next level. Much to my dismay, he left before my senior year to become the head wrestling coach at Drake University in Des Moines. I always thought it fitting that Coach ended up working at a school with a bulldog for its mascot. Here was a breed with which he shared an uncanny number of both physical and mental characteristics: stocky, muscular, determined, tenacious, and the heart of a fighter.

Such was my respect for Coach, and him for me, that when it came time to look at colleges my senior year, my folks and I accepted his invitation to visit his new school. More than anyone else, he convinced me that Drake would be a good fit for me. A few months later, I started my freshman year of college there.

During my enrollment at Drake, I focused my attention on academics. An 80-pound high school football player was one thing, but this was college. Not surprisingly, some of Coach's early recruits to his wrestling team were my buddies from Greenfield—guys like Mike Beaman, Donnie Wilson, and Greg Gruss, the latter two eventually becoming my roommates.

After four years, I graduated from Drake and moved out of state. For a few years after that I didn't see much of Coach. But then Melissa and I relocated back to the Midwest. Early in the season, Coach would bring his wrestling team to a tournament in the Chicago area, where we lived. He would make a point of calling me a few weeks before they were coming to make sure we had time to get together and reminisce. By this time, I was a university professor, and in his own subtle way he made it clear he was as proud of me as if he had been my own father.

Sadly, Coach Lonnie Timmerman passed away at the young age of fifty-eight in 1995. For me, whether in life or in death, he will always be just "Coach."

Courtesy of The Sidey Collection®

REJECTION AND REDEMPTION

Meet the Tigers

"Coach Channing Hall said Gary never missed a practice, loved to play basketball, and was a pleasure to coach."

From the *Adair County Free Press*, March 13, 1968

Gary Porter in State Track Meet

"Gary Porter was the only Greenfield trackman to qualify for the state meet in district competition at Villisca May 10. He ran the two-mile run in 11:00.7."

From the *Adair County Free Press*, May 22, 1968

The first snippet requires some reading between the lines: "[He] never missed a practice...was a pleasure to coach." Translation: He didn't see much playing time. The second one requires no reading between the lines. The stopwatch doesn't lie.

We had a bright orange basketball hoop bolted to the stand-alone garage behind our house. The basket started out with a net, but the net was eventually a casualty of the harsh winter weather. For hours on end, I shot free throws, practiced my set shot, drove the lane for an easy layup. Unlike most other sports, shooting baskets didn't require another kid. For me it was often a solitary pursuit. One day I was Bob Cousy, the little ball-handling magician with the Boston Celtics, the next day Rick Mount, the dead-on sharpshooter for the Purdue Boilermakers.

Of the Big Three in those days—baseball, football, and basketball—the last of these was my passion. Looking back, I don't have a plausible explanation. Maybe it was because I knew I couldn't hit a curveball, or for that matter ever catch up with a fastball. Maybe it was because I knew after one especially violent hit on the gridiron, one that knocked me senseless, that I wasn't meant to play football.

Once the snow started to fly and temperatures dropped, shooting baskets became more of a challenge, but in a way it was all the more rewarding. First, I had to shovel a path from the imaginary free throw line to the basket. The apron in front of the old garage wasn't paved, making shoveling down to the gravel even more work. But once a path had been cleared I was in business. The shots that went in were easy to retrieve; those that clanked off the rim ended up in a snow bank off to the side of my cleared path. This meant scraping a layer of snow off the old Spalding ball before returning to the free throw line. At times the frigid temperatures turned the ball hard as a rock, making any dribbling a real adventure. Not to worry, though. There was no referee blowing his whistle to charge me with traveling. My mind would start to wander.

Coach calls a time out. I just sunk a 20-foot set shot to tie the game. Fouled in the process. One second left in the state title game at Veterans Memorial Auditorium in Des Moines. It's up to you, Porter. Sink this free throw, and we're state champions. Miss it, we go to overtime.

One bounce. Bend the knees. Take a deep breath. Release the ball. The crowd holds its collective breath...

Eight years later. I was a senior in high school, only months away from going off to college. But I wasn't in the least concerned what that next step in my life might bring. What mattered to me, as it did to most teenage boys, was the here and now. Basketball season was in full swing, and I had one burning desire: to get off my relatively permanent seat on the bench for the GHS Tigers basketball team and assume my hard-earned spot on the hardwood floor. If not as a starter, then at least as someone seeing more than a few mop-up minutes at the end of blow-outs. After all, I worked as hard as anyone else on that team, had put in the hours shooting baskets by the old garage at the back of our house. How could I possibly be denied my rightful place on the floor?

After another Friday night gathering splinters on the bench, I finally got up enough courage. Enough to ascend the old tile stairway up to the second-floor locker room where I knew the coach would be sitting, pouring over shot charts, rebound differentials, and in every other way dissecting that night's game. The locker room emanated the dual odors of analgesic balm and sweat-soaked uniforms, not to mention the socks, jock straps, and other unseemly garments littering the floor.

And, yes, the courage it took to plead my case. Senior standing aside, you didn't just walk up to the coach and demand more playing time. I tried to be as diplomatic as a high school senior could be.

I feel I deserve a chance, Coach. I'm one of the best shooters on the team. You've seen me in practice. You know how reliable I am in the clutch.

I took a deep breath and waited for a response.

But there are others on this team who are quicker, others with more size, able to match up more physically with the brutes on the other team. I'll see what I can do—can't make any promises. There might be a chance to get you on the floor more in some upcoming games.

That's all I could have asked for, and I don't doubt that the coach meant it when he said he would see if he could get me some more minutes. As the season began to wind down, I did see a bit more action, but never cracked the starting lineup other than on Senior Night. The coach was right. I wasn't as fast as others. I wasn't as tall. But still, dreams die hard.

"Meet the Tigers" was a weekly feature in the *Free Press*, profiling each of the members of the basketball team. Early in the year, the stars were showcased; toward the end of the season it was a chance for the townsfolk to read about the subs, particularly the seniors soon to graduate. My profile was at the very end of the season. How do I know this? Because in the column next to my picture was the headline, "Tigers Dropped 51-58 in District." In other words, the last game of the season. The box score accompanying the story shows that I netted two field goals, went 0-1 from the foul line, and committed three personal fouls. The two stars on our team each scored 18 points.

Fast forward one month. Graduation was only a few weeks away, and I turned to the track. When I say "the track," I am being generous with the term. The reality is that our school didn't have a real oval, not even one of the cinder variety that were in use back then. What we had were a series of wooden stakes set out in the grass around the football field, meant to approximate 440 yards for each lap (long before the metric system made its way to the U.S.).

Being born with slow-twitch fibers had its obvious disadvantages on a basketball court and was of no use to a sprinter either. But as a long-distance runner, I fit the bill: slight of build, slow, and not terribly coordinated. I suspect, too, that I was drawn to the lure of the lonely long-distance runner. A future accountant if there ever was one.

By default, I was the Tigers' long-distance runner—our only miler, all the others possessing what they considered to be more common sense. Why punish yourself over a mile when you could compete at much shorter distances—100 yards, 200 yards, or at the most the quarter mile? Or better yet, why not skip the track altogether and join the golf team?

Prior to 1968, my senior year, the mile was the longest distance Iowa prepsters ran on a track. But all this changed that spring when the two-mile run was added. For a reason that escapes me all these years later, I never ran the two-mile during our regular outdoor season. It wasn't until the district meet in Villisca that I ran the first two-mile in Greenfield High School history. In fact, as they say, you can look it up. On the basis of that inaugural run at the district meet, I was the proud owner of the school record in the two-mile run. Never mind my record didn't stand all that long—I did, in fact, hold it.

Not only did I hold the record (guess you couldn't say I *broke* the record, since there wasn't one to break), I ran fast enough in that district meet to qualify for the state meet. A few weeks later, the track coach and I traveled up to the small town of Holstein in the northwest corner of the state for my appearance in the state meet. I was the only member of the track team to qualify in any event.

Rejection? Yes. I never led our basketball team to the state tournament at Vets Auditorium in Des Moines. And I finished in the middle of the pack at the state track meet, not worthy of a medal.

But on that lovely spring evening in Villisca, Iowa, the scrawny kid with the slow-twitch fibers did, in fact, redeem himself.

Courtesy of The Sidey Collection®

HUGH

"People ask me how I can keep up an interest in my home town. My answer is that I never really left and I have never found a substitute worthy of the name."

From the *Adair County Free Press*, September 11, 2002. Hugh Sidey in a letter to the editor to thank those greeting him on his seventy-fifth birthday.

A few years back, Douglas Bauer, a native of Prairie City, Iowa, penned a beautiful novel: *The Book of Famous Iowans*. It is the haunting tale of a young boy in the 1950s who watches his mother's illicit affair play out in their small town. The book's title is a bow to the boy's eccentric grandmother's hobby. She keeps a scrapbook of famous people from the Hawkeye State. Applying her own form of logic, the old lady has one cardinal rule for inclusion: a person must move away from Iowa to be truly famous.

Granted, most famous Iowans achieved their celebrity status beyond the boundaries of the two great rivers. Some of these celebrities were born not far from Greenfield. Just down the road, Corning can legitimately proclaim "Here's Johnny"—as in the famous late-night host Johnny Carson. The Duke, John Wayne in real life, was born in a small house in Winterset, our neighbor to the east. That town can also boast that it is the seat of the famous Madison County, thanks to some old, rickety bridges, a book, and a movie. Bob Feller, the flame-throwing Hall of Famer, hailed from Van Meter, barely a fast ball away from Winterset. Our thirty-first president, Herbert Hoover, was born and raised in West Branch, Iowa. Finally, ten miles down the road from Greenfield, our tiny neighbor of Orient can claim Henry Wallace, FDR's vice president, as a native son.

Sadly, my hometown birthed no presidents, no vice presidents, no Hollywood celebs, and no Hall of Famers. But we can count as one of our own a man who *chronicled* the presidents, beginning with Ike and continuing on down through George W. Bush.

Hugh Sidey was born into the newspaper business. The *Adair County Free Press*, a.k.a. "the paper," was started by the Sidey family all the way back in 1889. As kids, Hugh and his brother, Ed, started out sweeping floors and whatever else was needed to produce the weekly paper that in so many ways was the lifeblood of our small town.

Hugh earned a degree in journalism from Iowa State after serving in the post-World War II Army for eighteen months. He worked for the paper during the summer of 1950, then left Greenfield for good. Ed never did, running the paper until the day he died. According to Ed, that summer working for the *Free Press* was one of the happiest times of Hugh's life. Ironically, his departure coincided with my arrival in Greenfield, at the brand-new Adair County Hospital on the east side of town. It is likely that one of Hugh's assignments that summer was reporting on the progress being made on the construction of the hospital.

Both my wife and I were privileged to hear Hugh speak at conferences during our professional careers. It was a proud day for me to explain—between bites of rubbery chicken—that the fellow up onstage regaling thousands of accounting professors about his time with the presidents was from my hometown. I will never forget how down-to-earth and sincere Hugh was when I went up to the podium after his talk to explain our common bond.

My only regret is that I never had the chance to talk to Hugh on our home turf. Those who knew him best said he loved to come home and walk the streets of Greenfield, getting even more pleasure strolling down the alleys. If only I could have walked those alleys with him. Sure, I would have asked him what it was like to swim with JFK, to chat with LBJ aboard Air Force One, to cover the unfolding of Watergate. But I suspect before long we would just be two town kids back home, marveling at the beauty of the old oak trees, the emerald-green grass, and the tidy, white frame houses. We would eventually make our way up to our beloved town square, stopping to chat with the merchants as they greeted us. We might have even strolled out to the lake and asked one of the old-timers what was biting.

Hugh died suddenly in 2005 at the age of seventy-eight. He was surrounded by family while dining in a favorite Paris restaurant. Was it tragic that he should pass so far from home and the country he wrote about for over fifty years? I don't think so. Because, as Hugh said on the occasion of his seventy-fifth birthday, he never really left his hometown. And contrary to Thomas Wolfe's opinion, Hugh knew in his heart that you really can go home again, even if you are a continent away. All you have to do is close your eyes, listen for the chirping of the first robins of spring, recall the smell of freshly mown grass, and savor the first bite of a ruby-red apple.

Does Hugh Sidey qualify as a famous Iowan? Does he belong in a scrapbook with Johnny, the Duke, Bob, Herbert, and Henry? I suspect it depends on who is keeping the scrapbook. He is in mine, albeit nothing more than a manila folder into which I have tossed clippings, many of them from the *Adair County Free Press*.

In that letter to the editor to celebrate his seventy-fifth birthday, Hugh concluded:

"So long as I live I will keep my ties to the old home, come back as long as my legs will carry me and walk its beautiful streets where I grew up and where my spirit has always resided."

For me, those are the heartfelt words of a famous Iowan.

SPARKY NEVER LOST HIS SPARK

Saddle Club Has Nice Day for 1st Show

"Bright sunshine combined with warm temperatures provided an ideal spring day Sunday for the annual Ribbon Show staged by the Adair County Saddle Club as a 'warm up' session in preparation for the coming season. The event was held at the fairgrounds in Greenfield....Following are the ribbon winners as placed by Leo Wissler of Stuart, judge of the show:

"Western Pony (not over 14 and not under 46"):
1. 'Sparky' shown by Gary Porter of Greenfield;..."

From the *Adair County Free Press*, May 5, 1965

When we travelled to horse shows around the state of Iowa, we always took a cooler for pop. The name people use for carbonated beverages has always been a way to narrow down the part of the country they are from. It gives one away just as much as a Southern drawl or a Boston accent. Growing up in Iowa, those beverages were always "pop," not "soda."

Our cooler always contained two types of pop: 7 Up and Pepsi. The 7 Up served as a mixer for the adults, a way to concoct a "Seven and Seven"—or "highballs," as they called them. The Pepsi was for us kids. And one bottle was for our pony, Sparky. This, of course, was a time when pop came in glass bottles.

Sparky loved Pepsi. Not Coke, just Pepsi. When you put it up to his nose he would grab the bottle with his teeth. You held the bottom of the bottle, to stay clear of those big teeth, and let him go at it. Sure, a little of the Pepsi was wasted—the tops of those bottles were meant for human consumption, not equine enjoyment. But nonetheless, Sparky would suck down a good share of one of those 12-ounce bottles and then whinny his satisfaction.

Sparky was a constant, a part of daily life from my earliest childhood memories. Many of the early lessons I learned in life came from my horse-loving mother, with Sparky as her teacher's aide. She taught me how to ride. *Sit up straight in the saddle. Use your legs to balance. Eyes straight ahead.*

I learned how to groom a horse, using a curry comb to straighten Sparky's mane. Some of the lessons were less glamorous but no less important. I learned how to use a pitchfork to sift the manure from the straw and pitch the remains into a wagon. Most of all, Sparky taught me how to care for an animal.

Not a purebred, Sparky was either a big pony or a small horse. Enough to give a human an identity complex, but he wasn't the sort to dwell on such trivialities. We thought of him as a pony because that is how we showed him. The heights of ponies and horses are measured in "hands," with 4 inches making up one hand. Most pony classes required the steed be less than 14.2, meaning 14 hands and 2 inches in height. Sparky pushed the boundaries. During the show season, we had to keep his feet trimmed short enough to keep him under the maximum height for pony classes.

Certain events are forever cemented in your mind, regardless of how many or how few details about the event you can conjure up. As a town family, we didn't have our own barn. We rented the old barn across the alley from our house. There were a few stalls to keep the horses warm in the dead of winter, but otherwise they grazed in the pasture just to the east of the barn. All these years later I could walk to where that pasture used to be and accurately point to a spot within 20 feet of where "it" happened.

The event emblazoned in my memory took place early in Sparky's life with our family.

Doc Bricker, our family veterinarian, showed up with the tools of his trade in hand. By the time he left that pasture, Sparky had changed. He had been transformed from a stallion to a gelding. According to Webster, a "gelding" is a castrated male horse. Sparky was unfazed. He could have cared less what Webster had to say.

Transforming Sparky was a necessity if he were to be shown. The classes we entered were for geldings and mares, not stallions. Leave the studs back at the barn and let them do their thing when it came time to breed. Nonetheless, even after his alteration Sparky still thought of himself as a stallion. Put him in the show ring and he strutted around like he was a thoroughbred waiting to enter the starting gates at Churchill Downs. The challenge was calming him down enough to walk, trot, and canter at the judge's direction. When he did chill out, he was a charmer in the ring, and we took home many a blue ribbon and a few trophies as well.

When I went off to college, Sparky was there to say good-bye. And whenever I came back home, I always made sure to stop by his stall and give him a good scratching behind his ears. I remember the day when the call came from Dad that Sparky had passed on, somewhere around the ripe old age of twenty-eight.

And I can also recall that, in all those years, Sparky never lost his spark—nor did he ever lose his fondness for Pepsi.

Courtesy of The Sidey Collection®

POOL HALL

"Left ball in the corner pocket."

From the movie *Neighbors*, 1981

One of the ways we remember is by association, by making a connection. For me, those words from this movie will always be connected to our Pool Hall. The movie starred John Belushi as the mild-mannered suburbanite Earl Keese. Earl's wacky neighbor is played by Dan Aykroyd, and his equally wacky wife is played by Cathy Moriarty. In one scene, Aykroyd's character, "Captain" Vic, and his wife, Ramona, show up at Belushi's house for a game of pool. Prior to sending a pool ball careening across the room, Ramona calls out, "Left ball in the corner pocket." Needless to say, the slightly uptight character played by Belushi is not amused.

Long before the fictional Earl Keese took the screen, I knew the real-life Earl Keese. Earl's son, Gary, was a buddy of mine from the time his family moved from their farm to town, just up the street from us. Gary Keese and I spent many a summer afternoon locked in epic battles of home run derby, the hedge in his backyard serving as a stand-in for the Wrigley Field ivy and a Wiffle ball and bat as our tools of the trade.

Earl came to town to run the Pool Hall. I always felt a bit privileged, a quasi-insider, being friends with the son of the proprietor of this fine establishment. However, Earl was just as distraught as the fictional Earl Keese when one of us young whipper snappers sent a ball careening off the table. *Damn boys, try to keep those balls on the table, would you! You break a window, who is going to pay for it?*

I never knew the place by any other name—always just the Pool Hall. It wasn't called the Keese Pool Hall, nor did it sport some cutesy name like Earl's Eight Ball and Eatery. It was just the Pool Hall. I suspect it did have a name, probably for insurance and tax purposes, but such trivial details meant nothing to us kids.

I approached the Pool Hall from the alley, specifically the one on the northeast corner of the square. I used the back door for sheer convenience, as it was in the nearest alley coming from our house on the north edge of town. Others came in that same back door so as not to broadcast their arrival at the Pool Hall.

The Pool Hall wasn't the only place in town where billiards could be played. Most of the beer joints had a table, but they were undersized and cramped into tight quarters, players constantly ramming their cues into bar stools too close to the table. This, of course, didn't go over too well for the patrons trying to enjoy a glass of PBR at the bar. No such problems at the Pool Hall.

The size of the tables was only one of many differences between the Pool Hall and the beer joints sprinkled around the town square. Another was the form of refreshments. The taverns obviously served up alcoholic beverages, primarily beer and mixed drinks. Seven and seven, rum and Coke—these were two of the popular choices. No one would have ordered a glass of chardonnay in the beer joints. Or a pinot noir for that matter.

Because the taverns served alcohol, they were *legally* off limits to us youngsters. The Pool Hall was a different story. The establishment didn't serve alcohol. The closest you could come to a buzz was a Mountain Dew. Because they didn't serve alcohol, there was no minimum age for entering the Pool Hall. The only restriction imposed was typically the one set by parents. Some were more liberal in this regard than others. My Catholic mother tended toward the conservative side, not officially sanctioning my admittance until a later age than some of my buddies. Ironically, Gary Keese's mother, the wife of the proprietor, was just as devout a Catholic as my mother.

So if the Pool Hall didn't serve liquor, why was it off limits to some of us kids? My hunch is that it had to do with the twin evils of tobacco and language. Back then, most of our parents smoked, but that didn't mean they wanted their kids taking up the habit—or worst yet, learning to chew and spit. Regardless of when the link between smoking and cancer was first known, it was a dirty habit, not to be condoned for youngsters. The best way to discourage the use of nicotine was to make the Pool Hall off limits. The effects of secondhand smoke were nowhere near our radars, and if they had been it would have been another reason to forbid us kids from entering this smoky haven. A filmy haze, the kind you could cut with a knife, hung over the pool tables.

The second of the twin evils was language. The vernacular spoken in the Pool Hall was not the English language we were learning in school. Certain words uttered in the pool hall after a bad shot were not in Webster's—and they certainly were not ones to repeat at home.

Being a dutiful son, and not one to take unnecessary chances with my weekly allowance, I obeyed my mother and stayed away from this supposed den of iniquity until I got the nod that it was okay to enter. I don't recall what age that was, or even if it was tied to reaching a certain milestone. But once I got the approval, a whole new world opened up for me. My education in eight-ball etiquette began.

Before long I began noticing that every so often some of the grownups would disappear for a few minutes into the back room. I have no *proof* of what went on back there, although I imagine it likely had to do with *proof*...whether that was of the 86, 90, or higher variety. My suspicion is that Misters Jack and Jim (surnames Daniels and Beam) were popular hosts in that back room.

So unlike the beer joints in town, the Pool Hall did not *sell* alcohol. But another distinction between them was the food. The beer joints served up greasy cheeseburgers, and some of them, such as Mac's Tavern, even made pizzas. The cuisine available at the Pool Hall was more limited—no hot entrees on the menu. The standard fare consisted of candy bars, potato chips, and an assortment of nuts available at the front counter. Purchases were on the honor system. This meant that if Earl wasn't sitting in the front, you grabbed a bag of chips or peanuts, set your money down on the counter, and went back to your game of pool.

Next to the counter was the pop machine, where you could buy a Mountain Dew, a Dr. Pepper, a Pepsi, or a 7 Up. Some guys were the adventurous sort, combining their food and beverage purchases, mixing a bag of peanuts with their Pepsi. Drop the nuts in the pop, give it a good shake, and watch it fizz up. If you happened to be in the Pool Hall on a Saturday morning, you might opt for a carton of chocolate milk—"moo juice," as we called it—which was also available in the pop machine.

I haven't mentioned it yet, probably because it seems so obvious as to not require any explanation. But just in case. Ladies did not come in the Pool Hall. Don't misunderstand. I don't mean to imply that only females of questionable morals entered the place. There was no distinction based on the social standing of members of the opposite sex. *Females* simply did not go in the Pool Hall. This was before the revolution. "You've come a long way, baby," was still a few years away. Nor was age of any consequence. Young girls never came in the Pool Hall either, unless an occasional teenager stuck her head in the front door to persuade her boyfriend it was time to catch a movie across the way at the Grand.

Now to the games themselves. The Pool Hall had two types of playing surfaces. First, there were the standard pool tables used for the game of eight ball. These were not coin-fed tables, the type that had already found their way into the taverns. One of the allures of the Pool Hall was that you were waited on. Say a table opens up and you and your buddy are next in line. In anticipation, you have already selected your favorite cue from the rack on the back wall. Pound the butt end of your cue to the old wooden floor and holler, *Rack 'em up, Jonesy* (Jones being the last name of Earl's right-hand man).

The game of eight ball was very straightforward, perfect for beginners. Your buddy breaks and sinks the orange five ball. That means he has solids, since the balls numbered one through seven are solid in color. That leaves you with stripes, the balls numbered nine through fifteen. First one to pocket all his balls goes for the black eight ball. If you scratched—that is, you allowed the white cue ball to find its way into one of the pockets—you lost the game. Were this to happen, it would result in some of that language not learned in English class down at the school.

The other tables were reserved for the pros. These were the snooker tables. A snooker table looked like a stretched-out pool table, with even smaller pockets. Above the snooker table was strung a horizontal wire, running the length of the table. On the wire were wooden pegs that were used to keep score. For example, the blue ball was worth five points. If you sunk it, you got the satisfaction that came from taking your pool cue and slapping five wooden pegs briskly across the wire.

But the game of snooker was not for us rookies. You honed your skills at eight ball before you even thought of moving up to the snooker table. The old men who played snooker were revered by us youngsters. One of them was named Cal. When Cal was playing, you stopped your game of eight ball and took notice. You were watching a pro at work—the equivalent of Bart Starr on the gridiron, Bob Cousy on the hardwood, and Bob Feller on the mound. Like most of the kids, I did eventually work my way up to the snooker tables. That didn't mean I was in the same league as Cal and the other old-timers, but I could hold my own with the other youngsters.

Many a Saturday afternoon in the winter was spent in the Pool Hall, trading insults with my buddies, sipping a Mountain Dew, and inhaling secondhand smoke.

Rack 'em up, Jonesy. Left ball in the corner pocket.

Courtesy of The Sidey Collection®

BEFORE WALMART

*"A. P. Littleton opened the first store in the town,
in the first building which was erected in Greenfield.
This was a small structure, built of planks, and had been
used as a stage station. In June, 1859, he put in a small
stock of general merchandise in a front room. In the fall
of the same year he removed to a small building which
had been erected on a lot on the east side of the square."*

From *1915 History of Adair County Iowa and Its People*,
Lucian M. Kilburn, Supervising Editor

Growing up in Greenfield, there was no Walmart. There still isn't. You have to drive twenty miles south to Creston to find one, which no doubt many people in town do on a regular basis. Whether this is a good thing or a bad one is debatable and surely the topic of many lively conversations around town. I am a native, but I long ago surrendered my right to pass judgment on the morality of the locals' shopping habits, being nearly five decades removed from my hometown. One of the important distinctions between being a native and being a local. But still, a native can reflect on life before Walmart, when virtually every want, need, and frivolity could be satisfied with a five-minute walk, even if you lived out in the northern "suburbs" like we did. Allow me to illustrate.

It's early afternoon on a late summer day and the town kid is bored. The dog days have set in, and the novelty of seeing how many trips can be made to the swimming pool in one afternoon has long worn off. I won't need to start my paper route for another couple hours. Mom hands me two shiny half dollars.

The Bartletts' cow has suddenly run dry, their chickens have gone on strike, and we need eggs and milk. A buck is just enough, so hurry along. I'll need milk and eggs to bake a chocolate cake…

Sure, Mom. Not a problem. Back in a flash.

I approach the square from the north and notice the little white hut that has been a fixture on this side of the square for years. Eddie is hard at work, popping corn and freezing ice for his snow cones. Eddie is confined to a wheelchair, but nothing ever dampens his spirits. Today is no different. He cheerfully greets me, and I am instantly tempted by the aroma of fresh buttered popcorn. I fish in my pocket for one of the half dollars. At a nickel a bag, this still leaves me with plenty for the groceries. I'll be back at this spot later in the afternoon when stacks of the *Des Moines Tribune* arrive and I peddle my paper route on my Schwinn bike.

I cross the street to hear Cliff Welcher whistling a tune as he rolls out the big awning over the storefront of Crooks Clothing. Cliff announces the high school football games and will soon be in action on Friday nights. I admire the Converse high tops in the window and let him know I will be back to try on a pair before the start of the basketball season. *They won't be on sale for Crazy Days next week, but stop by anyway. You never know what bargains we may set out on the sidewalk.*

I saunter on down the sidewalk and pause in front of the State of Iowa liquor store. This is where the hard stuff is sold—whiskey, vodka, gin, and so forth. Packaged liquor. Back then, if you wanted a six pack you visited the local tavern, but if you were looking for a fifth of whiskey you had to transact with the good folks in charge of the Hawkeye State. Better not gaze too long, or word could get back to the folks. Plus, I am distracted by the sounds emanating from the Pool Hall across the alley.

Colorful language can be heard, blending in with the melodic sound of a cue ball slamming into a full rack of fifteen. I step in the front door just long enough to say hello to my classmate's father, Earl Keese, the proprietor of the establishment. With a half bag of popcorn left, I suddenly realize how well a Mountain Dew would go with it. Earl rings me up and I hand him a nickel. I glance over to see that a table has just opened up and figure I have just enough time for a quick game of eight ball with Earl's son, Gary. I place a dime on the felt cushion and wait for Jonesy to rack 'em up. Three games later and thirty cents lighter, I decide it isn't my day and move on.

I continue down the sidewalk on the east side of the square. Dick Gross is simultaneously cutting hair and holding court down below Eckardt's Shoes. Seeing him reminds me that I will need my flattop trimmed a bit before the start of the school year. Around the corner stands Sinner Motor Co. It's the end of the season, and the new models will soon be arriving. Sale signs hang from the Falcons, Fairlanes, and Thunderbirds lined up in the showroom. I am tempted to take a look, but I resist. Better get to those eggs and milk.

I cross the street and look in the big windows of The Golden Rule. The mother of another classmate, Curt Weber, is working today. Wilma is a fixture at the ladies' department store, and she hollers out to be sure to say hello to my mom. *Sure will, Wilm. And you tell Curt hey. See him soon for football practice.*

Next door is Fry's Rexall Drug. My better judgment tells me that after downing a bag of popcorn and a Mountain Dew, I probably don't need much more, but the temptation is too hard to resist. I belly up to the soda fountain and order a root beer float, a cherry on top please. I slap a shiny dime down on the counter, work the float down as far as possible with a spoon, and then use a straw to slurp the froth from the bottom.

As I head out, I hear some of the patrons next door at Mac's Tavern debating the pressing issues of the day.

Too damn much rain lately, can't even get a tractor in the fields.

Shoot Harold, lighten up. Most years you're bitching about a drought.

From the other end of the bar: *The Hawkeyes will be lucky to win half their games this fall, you mark my words.*

I'll take your money, Clyde. That team is loaded for bear this year.

Now that I am already around on the south side of the square, I may just as well circle on around to the grocery store, no need to retrace my steps. I see Gil Wallace sitting behind the counter in The Music Box. "Daddy O," we call him. He spots me and beckons me in. *Hey, little buddy. Chuck Berry's latest just came in. Man, can that cat belt it out. Can you dig it?* I see the clock on the wall and reckon I will have to dig it at a later date. *See you later, gator.*

I hustle around to the west side of the square. A sign hangs over one of the storefronts, announcing the upstairs offices for Dr. King, our family dentist. I am reminded that before long I will be paying him a visit and probably hearing a lecture about the evils of too many bags of popcorn, all those bottles of Mountain Dew, and maybe one too many root beer floats.

But when you are a bored town kid, your attention span sometimes approaches that of a two-year-old. I am now standing in front of Wiig's Store and thinking a handful of lemon drops and maybe a couple jaw breakers would hit the spot. Bobbi Wiigs takes my order and asks whether he can put those in a little sack for me, honey. Why not? We make an exchange, Bobbi handing me a white bag of hard candy and me forking over a dime from my pocket. Nothing like a good, old-fashioned jaw breaker to help pass the time. Sorry, Dr. King.

Just enough time, I'm thinking, to walk to the corner, buy Mom's milk and eggs, and head home. I step inside Berg's Sure Save Market, and Delphine Jensen greets me at the cash register. She delivered a baby boy in the new hospital a few days before I was born, and I never pass up the opportunity to chide her that Mom and I were shut out from all the accolades and press that came her way. I hurry to the coolers in back and grab the milk and eggs. Delphine rings me up. *Ninety-five cents, young man. And with five thrown in for Uncle Sam, that will be a buck on the nose.*

I reach in my jeans pocket and suddenly have a sinking feeling. Not one directly attributable to the popcorn, pop, ice cream, and candy, but a connection nonetheless. I may not be a day late, but I'm sure as heck a dime short and then some of what it is going to take for a gallon of milk and a dozen eggs. In fact, I pull the remains from my pocket and see that I am *six* dimes short!

Now what? My sin may not be mortal, but I'm guessing it may be good for at least five Our Fathers and ten Hail Marys come Saturday afternoon in the confessional. Stealing from your mother to satisfy your worldly pleasures. And then thinking of devising a lie to cover your tracks. Time for some quick thinking.

Delphine, I'll be back in a minute. I gotta go in the back and check on something.

There I find Bernie Berg hunched over his desk, an island surrounded by produce crates and boxes of canned goods yet to be shelved. Bernie and I don't have a written contract, but a gentlemen's agreement, a handshake, that I will deliver him sweet corn from my garden plot at a going rate of 25 cents a dozen.

What can I do for you, young man?

Uh, just wondering, Mr. Berg, if I might impose on you for an overnight advance on that sweet corn I am bringing in tomorrow. What the heck, I figure. Another sin of the venial variety should only cost me a few more Our Fathers and Hail Marys. So here I go.

There must be a hole in these ratty old jeans. I seem to have lost the buck I had for my milk and eggs.

Bernie didn't just fall off the turnip truck, and he gives me a look that says, "We both know better, but okay, you had a hole in your jeans. I can advance you the price of a few dozen ears of corn."

Sounds good, kid. Just tell Delphine we talked. Now beat it. I got work to do.

I have been saved. If I hustle home, I can drop off the milk and eggs in time to turn around, get back uptown, and deliver newspapers. Plus, I'm already starting to recover from all that popcorn, pop, ice cream, and candy. Mom's chocolate cake sure is going to hit the spot tonight.

Courtesy of One Hundred Fifty Years of History: Greenfield 1856-2006

YOUNG ENTREPRENEURS

"Eddie Bickford was born in 1931, with a severe birth defect. At the age of 15, he contracted polio. The combination left him with a severe physical handicap, but his positive attitude prevailed.

His father built the popcorn stand, after Eddie had graduated from GHS in 1950. For more than 35 years, during warm weather months, Eddie made and served each bag of fresh popcorn and sold Sno-cones."

From *One Hundred Fifty Years of History: Greenfield 1856-2006*

These days it is fashionable to be an entrepreneur. Your own man. Your own woman. Not tied down to a desk in a cubicle. Eddie Bickford was an entrepreneur long before it was fashionable. His popcorn stand on the north side of the square was a welcome sight to kids and grown-ups alike. Eddie always greeted you with a smile and waited patiently until you made your selections. *Hey Eddie! How about a cherry snow cone and a bag of buttered popcorn today?*

Back in the day, many town kids like Eddie were entrepreneurs. From an early age, I was one of them. I went into business, assuming risk in order to make money. I was an independent contractor—no 401(k), no profit-sharing. If there were any profits, they were mine to keep.

Ironically, this was years before I studied bookkeeping in high school and accounting in college, and long before I made the teaching of all this my life's work. Double entry had yet to enter my vocabulary, but that didn't stop me from meticulously tracking my finances.

One of my earliest endeavors had a connection to Eddie's Super Popcorn. I delivered newspapers, which the driver dropped directly behind Eddie's stand. We got our local news once a week, courtesy of the *Adair County Free Press* (still in operation to this day). The *Omaha World Herald* arrived from ninety miles to the west. Two other daily papers came out of Des Moines: the *Register* in the morning and the *Tribune* in the afternoon. Many years ago, the two Des Moines papers merged, and a single morning edition is now published.

Not being a morning person, I was happy to deliver the *Tribune*. As soon as the driver dropped the papers behind Eddie's stand, we would begin our work. Folding your bundle of papers so they all fit in your bag was part art, part science. Once this was done, I would throw the bag over my shoulder, mount my Schwinn bike, and start down the streets on my route. A snow cone or bag of popcorn from Eddie would have to wait. Once a week, I collected from my customers, making change from one of those metal coin dispensers attached to my belt.

Another of my early ventures was as a "lawn care specialist." I mowed yards. A John Deere riding mower was not in the equation, not when you were just starting out with little capital to invest in plant and equipment. Nor was my first mower self-propelled. Instead, I had a push mower. I not only pushed the mower around the lawns, I also pushed it around town to my different clients.

Most lawns in town were flat and didn't require any specific skills or the use of brute force to navigate. The yard at the Martin cousins' house just around the corner from our place was a different matter. To a young kid, the slope on the north side of their house was Mount Everest. After a number of falls and near misses in pinning myself under the blades of my mower, I reached the conclusion that I could benefit from some more traction by wearing my baseball cleats. It worked.

Probably the most entrepreneurial of all my enterprises was the time I spent in the "agricultural production" business. Just like the farmers out in the country, I assumed the risks related to the ever-changing Iowa weather when I planted a vegetable garden on the Galbreaths' open land to the north of our place. I don't recall now whether I entered into any sort of short-term seasonal lease of the land or whether the neighbors simply said, *Yeah, kid. Go ahead and plant your corn.* Most likely the latter.

My staple crop was good old Iowa sweet corn. It took some experimenting, but eventually I developed a knack for knowing when the corn was ready to be picked. I sold it to Bernie Berg, the owner of one of the two grocery stores on the square. How I set my prices and how often I delivered product to the grocery store I can't recall. Regardless, I must have made quite the impression on Bernie. A few years later, I had my first real taste of employment when he hired me to be a stock boy at 90 cents an hour.

My days as an entrepreneur had come to a close. Delivering newspapers, mowing yards, raising sweet corn—they all taught me important life lessons. Fold your papers so they all fit in your bag, wear your baseball cleats on a hilly yard, and pick your corn only when it is ripe. And, oh yes, save some spare change for a snow cone and a bag of popcorn at Eddie's.

PART II

Leaving

Personal Collection

D o we ever really *leave* home? My dad went off to fight in WWII and was one of those fortunate enough to return home after the war. But had he ever really left home, even when he was a world away in France and Germany?

Myself, I went off to college. But that first night in my dorm room, had I really left home? After college I left Iowa, only to return for brief visits. Back for happy and sad times, mostly weddings and funerals.

To me, it comes down to your definition of home. A house we can leave, as almost all of us do at some time in our lives. But home, that is something different. Home lives on forever in our hearts and in our minds. So contrary to what Thomas Wolfe may have thought, I truly believe you can go home. Just close your eyes, breathe in the aroma of fresh lilacs, and listen for the first robins in springtime.

You are home again, never to leave.

Personal Collection

END OF INNOCENCE

Best Wishes, Grads

*"It may seem a terrible drag to our young people to
live in a place where most of the community knows
your name and cares what you do. We predict that
later on, at a university campus of twenty or thirty
thousand students or at a job in a city of hundreds
or even thousands or perhaps millions of people, it
will mean a lot more to have grown up in such a place."*

From Ed Sidey's column in the *Adair County Free Press*, May 15, 1968

Innocence. The word suggests freedom, a lack of guilt. If you are
not guilty of some transgression, then you must be innocent. For
me, my lack of guilt, my innocence, was a product of both *where*
and *when* I grew up.

Growing up in rural Iowa in the fifties and sixties kept me
about as free from transgressions as one could imagine. (Only after
I got my driver's license did I indulge in the transgression that
lured many of us teenagers: circling the town square in the wrong
direction, late on a Saturday night.) At the same time, innocence of
a personal sort seems by its nature to be temporary, to be fleeting.
Something that eventually ends, forever lost. For me, the end of my

innocence didn't happen overnight, the result of some tragic event like the loss of a parent to cancer or a classmate to a head-on car crash. But it is pretty easy to trace it to a series of events—some of a personal nature, others on a larger stage—that occurred in 1968.

For me, that year stands out, towering high above all the others. When it began, I was halfway through my senior year at Greenfield High, a seventeen-year-old with very few cares in the world. What did concern me was not issues of a worldly sort. Instead, I worried about things like how to keep a clear complexion, what clothes to wear to look cool, how to break the starting lineup on the varsity basketball team, and how to talk Dad into letting me have the keys to the Olds 88. To say that my radar didn't extend much beyond the city limits of Greenfield would be an understatement.

I started the year not knowing for certain, but with a good suspicion, that it would be my last as a full-time *resident* of Greenfield. The term "resident" is probably a bit stilted for what I mean. Ask the folks in town, and it is unlikely any of them will say they think of themselves as residents. I never did. Greenfield was home, plain and simple. There was no need to think of it in any other terms.

Still, in a few months I would be moving away from the only house I had ever lived in, that two-story, white frame house at 205 NE Dodge. I had been admitted to Drake University and would be leaving in another eight months to start a completely new chapter in my life. I wasn't consciously looking to start a new chapter. My school years in Greenfield were great, and I never once dreamed what life would be like if and when I could somehow escape. There was nothing from which I wanted to escape. I just assumed I would go away to school and didn't give much thought to the consequences of that decision.

By many historians' standards, my graduation year of 1968 was one of the most significant years in the twentieth century. It was a year of killings, many of them in a distant land called Viet Nam. In late January, the Viet Cong launched the Tet Offensive. But for a high school senior planning to go to college, Viet Nam really didn't get my attention. Now, finding a way to somehow get more playing time on the Tigers basketball team, that was a different story.

The killings weren't limited to foreign soil. In April, Martin Luther King was struck down by an assassin's bullet in Memphis. Do I recall hearing about it? Sure, it was front-page news in the *Des Moines Register*. Most of us from that time can picture in our minds the motel balcony where the civil rights leader—who told us all, "I have a dream"—lost his life. But then track season was in full swing and most of my energy was focused on seeing how fast I could circle four times around a quarter-mile track.

In late May, the GHS class of '68—all sixty-two of us—sat in the bleachers in front of that quarter-mile track and listened as we were told we could make a difference, the universal message delivered to all grads. Live every day to the fullest. We flung our caps in the air, hugged each other, and promised to stay in touch. My cousin, Pam, and I looked the picture of contentment and confidence, adorned in our caps and gowns and ready to face the world and whatever it might hold for us. We were all bit players in a hit movie of that year—we were each *The Graduate*. "So here's to you, Mrs. Robinson."

In June, more gunshots, more violence. This time it was another Kennedy, JFK's younger brother Bobby. Four and a half years earlier a motorcade in Dallas—this time in a Los Angeles hotel. When the tragic news came, I was biding my time before going off to college. One last summer working at the fairgrounds—painting buildings, mowing grass, and working on my tan.

Maybe Viet Nam hadn't captured my full attention just yet, but it did for the thousands of protesters at the Democratic National Convention in Chicago that August. Mayor Daley called in the National Guard and television captured the violence that ensued. Shortly after that my cousin, Pat, dropped me at the front door of my new dorm, and I began a new chapter in my life. I was a college freshman, away from home for the first time and no longer confined to the boundaries of a town barely a mile square. Kids in the dorm came from faraway places, some from high schools the size of my entire hometown. Professors opened my eyes to a world far beyond any I had known about.

The monumental year of 1968 ended with Walter Cronkite narrating while our little sphere of a planet appeared out the window as a camera shot from astronauts circling the moon. After a year of killings, we seemed to be ending with a ray of hope for the future of our world. And it was an ending of a different sort for me—the end of my innocence.

Courtesy of The Sidey Collection®

GREENFIELD GOES
COLD TURKEY

*"My eight weeks in Iowa in the summer of 1969
directing* Cold Turkey *remain a highlight of my life.
When I was seeking Richard Brooks's advice about
whether to do it, he quoted Alfred Hitchcock as having
once said that no man could feel closer to playing God
than a director of a film on location. Think about that.
You are in Greenfield, Iowa, which you alone have
renamed Eagle Rock, to the township's great pleasure."*

From "Even *This* I Get to Experience" by Norman Lear, 2014

It happened in the summer of 1969, right after my freshman year
of college. Norman Lear had scoured the country looking for the
perfect place to film a comedy about an entire town challenged
to stop smoking for thirty days. Overnight, Greenfield became
the fictional Eagle Rock.

There was something about our town square that won Norman
Lear over. Other towns in the area, including Winterset, had bit
parts in the film, but Greenfield snatched the lead role. About
twenty-five years later, Winterset could claim its own stardom
thanks to those covered bridges and the likes of Clint Eastwood
and Meryl Streep. But Greenfield had its own star power in the

summer of 1969 when Dick Van Dyke, Bob Newhart, Tom Poston, Jean Stapleton, Pippa Scott, and a host of other Hollywood staples roamed the town square.

The plot was fairly straightforward. An ad exec, played by Bob Newhart, convinced a tobacco company that it could generate huge publicity with virtually no cost by offering a town a $25 million prize if its residents stopped smoking—went cold turkey—for thirty days. The scheme seemed foolproof, especially back in the 1960s when smoking was so much more prevalent and socially acceptable than it is today. How could an entire town stop smoking for any length of time, let alone one month? Dick Van Dyke played a preacher who took the lead in convincing the townspeople to quit smoking. A nonsmoker himself, the preacher even took up smoking to show his resolve and lead the effort.

That was Eagle Rock in the movie. Back in the real world of Greenfield, the idea was hatched at a city council meeting that the town should start its own cold-turkey campaign. The town's mayor—Dale Yount, a chain smoker himself—led the effort. Over one hundred residents signed up. My mother, always her own woman, was one of the holdouts, not willing to give up her Parliaments for the sake of conformity.

I did live at home that summer after my freshman year at Drake University. But I had taken a job with a pipeline company to mow right of ways and paint buildings. And because the filming took place in August and September, I was back in Des Moines when many of the scenes were shot. Plenty of friends, neighbors, and relatives did sign up as extras, basking in the glory of their town gone Hollywood. Eventually the filming ended, the cameras were packed, and the celebs returned to the West Coast. But they never forgot their time in Greenfield.

Many of those celebs came back for a reunion in 1999, including Norman Lear, Dick Van Dyke, Tom Poston, and Jean Stapleton. They were received as warmly as they had been thirty years earlier. But that many years later, not all the townspeople who experienced that magical time were still alive for the reunion. Very likely a few had passed on from the ill effects of nicotine.

Norman Lear returned to Greenfield again in 2014. He had a new book out and was invited to come and chat with the locals in the theater of the beautifully restored Warren Opera House. To his surprise, it was announced that the theater would from that day forward be known as the Norman Lear Theater. Teary eyed, Norman Lear fondly recalled that summer in Greenfield and what it meant to him. Incidentally, in the same year *Cold Turkey* was released, his TV series *All in the Family* began its nine-year run and became one of the most acclaimed sitcoms in the history of television.

As often happens in everyday conversation, someone will invariably ask, *Where ya from?* To place my hometown geographically, I answer, *Small town, sixty miles southwest of Des Moines.* But then I always add, *Did you ever see that movie about a whole town that decided to stop smoking? That's my hometown. Go rent the movie. You'll love it!*

So thanks, Norman Lear, for "discovering" Greenfield. You knew the real deal when you saw it. You knew ordinary folks weren't going to be starstruck by the likes of Bob and Dick, but would instead welcome them with open arms to their little town on the prairie.

THE DAY ELVIS DIED

*"Death Captures Crown of Rock and Roll—
Elvis Dies Apparently After Heart Attack"*

Headline from *The Commercial Appeal*,
a Memphis newspaper, August 17, 1977

The three of us look straight ahead, squinting into the August sun making its first appearance of the day. My girlfriend, Melissa—who would be my wife a year later—reminds us to smile for the camera. Flanking me on each side are my folks, both taking a break from work to say good-bye. Confirming the bright sun, our shadows line up behind us, relegated for now to the second row. I wear an unbuttoned red polo shirt, khaki jeans, and sandals. I also sport that air of confidence you might expect from a twenty-six-year-old fresh out of grad school, weeks away from my first appointment as an Assistant Professor at a school in San Diego. My long hair and moustache give me that seventies look, 1977 to be specific.

On my right, Dad also wears khaki jeans, but a more functional shirt—a button-down with a front pocket to hold his glasses case. My right arm over his shoulder, Dad folds one arm over the other in front of him, just as he might have stood at ease during his Army days in the Second World War. Mom is on my left, wearing a pair of yellow slacks with a matching cotton jacket. Her right arm is barely visible, most of it disappearing around my waist, her trying to hold on as long as she can.

While I wear a look of coolness, bordering on bravado, the expressions on their faces are more apprehensive, more tentative. Colorado, where I had attended grad school, was far enough from our Iowa home. But now…California. Within minutes Melissa and I will hop into my Ford Torino—its left rear fin just barely visible in the corner of the faded picture—and head west. In a bit of irony, my cousin, Pat, will join us, heading back to a military post in Denver. This isn't the first time he will be an accomplice to my leaving home. Not by design, but by being in the right place at the right time. Pat gave me a lift to Des Moines when I moved into the dorms at Drake University for my freshman year in the fall of 1968.

Check your oil, Dad reminds me as we head for the car.

Call for Ralph, from Mom as we pull away from the parking lot.

Dad's instructions are of a very practical sort, him being from that generation when every gas stop meant you instinctively lifted your hood and pulled the dipstick. Mom's directive is code. Before the days of emails, cell phones, and text messages, I always called person-to-person for Ralph when I reached my destination. Technically, it would be person-to-dog since Ralph was the family beagle. I would hear Mom on her end explaining to the operator that Ralph couldn't come to the phone, which wasn't precisely the case. The floppy-eared hound was capable of *coming* to the phone; it was just that, being of the canine persuasion, he couldn't *take* any calls. Mom would hear my reassuring voice on the other end saying I would try to reach Ralph later. She could go to sleep knowing all was well.

A final toot of the horn as we pull away and I point the Torino west. By mid-morning, we cross the Missouri River at Omaha and begin the long trek on I-80 across Nebraska. Lincoln, Kearney, North Platte, each a sign of encouragement that we are making progress. Even at seventy miles per hour it takes most of the afternoon to cross the Cornhusker State. The sun is now at full strength, bearing down on my driver's seat window.

The local AM station gives the midday market report: December corn up three points, January soybeans down ten, feeder cattle trading at $145 at the Omaha stockyards. No real need in hearing the obituary report sponsored by the local funeral home, I punch the FM button to pick up some music. Mostly country, I search a bit to find some rock and roll.

All these years later, I don't recall exactly where we were, only that I-80 seemed to go on forever. A somber voice came on the radio, breaking into the local programming. The King is dead. Found this afternoon in his Memphis home, Elvis is gone from this life at the age of forty-two. To a young buck in his mid-twenties, this was a middle-aged man. How foolish youth can be. To my parents, then in their mid-fifties, Elvis was a youngster.

This may not have been the day the music died. That was many years earlier, when Buddy, Richie, and the Big Bopper met their fate in an Iowa cornfield. But August 16, 1977, was a day everyone from my generation will remember—where they were, what they were doing, how they heard the news.

Sometime later that day, Melissa and I pull into Boulder after dropping off my cousin in Denver. I call person-to-person for Ralph, but alas, he has stepped out for the evening. *You'll have to try later,* I am told. We spend a few days packing up, saying good-bye to the place where we first met just a year earlier.

More driving now, but this time on a diagonal southwest to southern California. Eventually we arrive in San Diego, eager to start the next chapter in our lives together. I am a freshly minted Ph.D., ready to begin a career in academia. Melissa accepts a sales position with Big Blue, pedaling IBM typewriters up and down the streets of San Diego.

On a Saturday in late October, I proposed over a duck dinner and a bottle of champagne. We decided we would make the announcement to our families when we were both home in a couple of months.

All these years later, I stare at the photo. Beyond the obvious story any picture tells, how much can you read into a snapshot? I suppose as much as you want, as much as you need to in order to make sense of things. Was Mom really holding on, somehow knowing, sensing this might be our last day together? I have no reason to suspect this to be the case. But the longer I look at the photo, the three of us begin to slowly fade to the background and our shadows take center stage.

Ray C. Strang, Slow Poke, © *NYGS 1945, 1973*

SLOW POKE AND
THE DAVENPORT

*"The Greenfield community was saddened and
shocked early this Wednesday morning when
it was learned that Helen Porter had passed
away suddenly at 9:30 p.m. Tuesday, Nov. 1,
several hours after being admitted into
the Adair County Memorial Hospital.*

*"She had followed her normal routine during
the day and became suddenly ill at her home.
For nineteen years she had served as the efficient
bookkeeper at the G. & H. motor freight lines.*

*"For several years she had served as
secretary of the Adair County Fair."*

From the *Adair County Free Press*, November 2, 1977

Are you sitting down? came the voice of my brother on the other
end of the phone, half a question and half a suggestion that if I
wasn't I should be. He was calling from back home in Iowa with
the news of the death earlier that evening of our fifty-four-year-old
mother. She had been in good health, having ridden her horse just
days before. Mom came home from work, mentioned to Dad she
didn't feel well, and lay down on the davenport. Before long, Dad

was driving her to the local hospital, and not long after that she was gone. A woman who died much too young—but as a devout Catholic, it was only fitting it would be on All Saints' Day.

When I was growing up, our family owned a davenport. This was probably a reflection of where we lived—1950s Iowa. It served the same purpose as a sofa or a couch, but it was always called a "davenport." The same way we drank pop, not soda. The davenport sat in the living room of our white, wood-framed, two-story house on Dodge Street. The room was a *living* room, not a family room, and certainly not a great room. It was a living room because that was where so much of the life of our family played out. And the davenport was the center of all the living that took place in this room. It was where I sat and held hands with my future wife when I first brought her home to meet the family. It was where, as a little kid, I sprawled out to watch Saturday morning cartoons on our black-and-white TV set. And it was where the woman who will always be a saint to me lay down in our house for the last time on that fateful first day of November 1977.

Above our davenport hung a picture. It depicted a western scene with a cowboy mounted on his trusty gray horse, looking back to encourage a young colt to hurry along. Rocky buttes framed the background for the scene, with a field of yellow wildflowers in the foreground. Above the buttes, soft white clouds hung in the sky like giant pillows. The little bay colt, with a white star on its forehead, was the inspiration for the title of the painting: *Slow Poke*. For anyone who knew Mom, it would be no surprise that she would pick a cowboy painting to hang in her living room. She grew up riding her pony to a one-room country schoolhouse, and she remained a cowgirl her entire life. During the time before cigarette ads were banned, she used to kid about the handsome Marlboro Man. I suspect that when Mom glanced up at the painting, that cowboy reminded her of that famous Madison Avenue creation.

Dad stayed in the house for many years after Mom died. But inevitably, the steps to the second floor became an issue and he reluctantly made the decision to move to a one-story complex for seniors on the other end of town. The only house my parents ever owned—the one that was in our family nearly fifty years— was put up for sale. And of course, the requisite yard sale soon followed—the one that accompanies any move from a house to an apartment.

I can vividly recall the beautiful October afternoon of the sale. Leaves had begun to fall from the old oak and elm trees in our yard, some of the same trees that had served as witnesses to, as well as active participants in, games of baseball and hide-and-seek during my youth. A lunch of sloppy joes, potato chips, and homemade pie was provided for the townsfolk, many of whom showed up at these auctions not because they needed to add to their own accumulation of stuff, but out of respect for a good neighbor or friend. Myself, I made the trip home with the announced intention to lend whatever help I could to the work of the day. Of course, in my heart I knew full well that I was there just as much because I needed to be. I needed to see home one last time, to be able to lock it permanently in my mind.

I arrived early and before long found myself eyeing the merchandise scattered around the yard. Dad had made it clear I could pull out just about anything, but I shouldn't tarry. In other words, "Speak now, or forever hold your peace." I certainly wasn't in the market for a davenport and can't honestly even tell you whether it was on the auction block that day. But out of the corner of my eye, I spotted it—or to be more precise, him. There was *Slow Poke*, and before long he would be someone else's property. In fact, the picture would be just that—a piece of property, no memories attached. Needless to say, *Slow Poke* was quickly tucked away in our SUV and will forever be in the family. As a source of solace and inspiration, it now hangs across from my desk in our home.

A few years ago, I sat at that desk, staring at a blank computer screen. As often happens, I found myself drawn to the picture. In the lower right-hand corner, I noticed for the first time the artist's name in simple block letters: S T R A N G. I glanced back at the empty computer screen and without any hesitation Googled "Slow Poke and Strang." Within seconds I became connected to the artist who had created this picture that meant so much to me. AskART.com told me Ray C. Strang was born in 1893 and was wounded during World War I. After coming home, he had a successful career as an illustrator and painter of traditional western cowboy scenes.

Soon, my Googling led to even more revelations. I found an interview with Robert Earl Keen[1], a Texas singer/songwriter. The interview, conducted by Arthur Wood, followed the release of Keen's album, *A Bigger Piece of Sky*. The cover art for the album was—you guessed it—none another than Ray Strang's *Slow Poke*. There on the computer screen, on the cover of the album, was the same image as the one hanging on the wall in front of me. The

---

1 Recently, Melissa and I were fortunate to see Robert Earl Keen in concert. And even luckier to be able to meet him backstage after the show. I explained our common connection and handed him a copy of this very essay. I hope he enjoyed it and felt he had a kindred spirit.

interviewer asked Keen if he owned the original. Turns out he didn't own the original any more than I did. He explained that he owned a print of it, one that had hung above his grandmother's bed. She had lived in an old house out in western Texas, and when she died they asked him what he wanted. He gave the same response I did that day back at the yard sale: He wanted the print for its sentimental significance. And when it came time to put an image on *A Bigger Piece of Sky*, he decided on *Slow Poke*.

Years have passed since the day of that yard sale back home in Iowa. Even more have gone by since Robert Earl Keen recorded his album. Add a few more years to go back to that day when Mom lay down for the last time on the davenport, and quite a few more to when she rode across the countryside on her pony to the one-room schoolhouse. All I have to do to bring back those memories is glance up at the picture in my office. If I really focus on the scene, I find myself back home, sitting on the davenport. And suddenly the cowboy on the gray horse is replaced by a cowgirl. She is looking back over her shoulder, not at a little colt but at a young cowpoke, with a gentle reminder to him: *No need to sit down. Come along now.*

PART III

Longing

Courtesy of The Sidey Collection®

Longing for times past is fraught with danger, warning signs all around. Things change. Favorite uptown stores shutter their windows. Some friends gray, others go bald. Loved ones die, and there are more names recognizable on the gravestones in the cemetery on the edge of town than on the buildings up on the square. And now there is talk of "consolidating" counties. No, nothing seems to stay the same—except the march of time.

But looking back is not all for naught. It is what allows us to honor those now residing in that cemetery up on the hill. And to talk over the old times with those of us fortunate enough to still recall those days. And to remember that magical ride on the Ferris wheel, when it stopped at the top and the lights of the town sparkled on the landscape below.

Every time I go back to my hometown and walk the streets, I am reminded of my youth—of those endless summer days when my world consisted of a patch of ground called Greenfield.

Courtesy of The Sidey Collection®

BORN ON A FRIDAY

*"Mr. and Mrs. Dick Porter announce the arrival of
an eight pound son, Friday morning at the new hospital.
Mrs. Myrtie Porter of Greenfield and William Fagan of
Stuart are grandparents. He has been named Gary Allen."*

From "Stork Notes" in the *Adair County Free Press*, September 14, 1950

There was the evidence. In black and white, literally. It told me I
was born on a Friday, in the morning to be more precise.

I was paying a visit to the *Adair County Free Press* to pour
over the huge, dusty, unwieldly books containing issues of the
local paper going back over a century—long before I called the
place home.

Linda Sidey told me to have at it—pull out any and all issues
and take a look. I began opening these books, turning the pages
as carefully as possible, not wanting to leave my imprint on these
tomes that—week after week, year after year—have dutifully
recorded the history of our town. Each book represented a
year in the life of the community—a life that included births,
deaths, weddings, divorces, sports scores, local elections, and
movie listings. And, of course, the weather, which is crucial
to a town as dependent on agricultural as ours. Plus the ads
for the local establishments. Ads for businesses that have long

since passed from the collective memories of most of the current townsfolk. But businesses that served the community well. I discovered that Greenfield, a town of 2,000, once boasted no less than four showrooms selling the newest models of automobiles: Sinner Ford, Kirlin Dodge, Schildberg Chevrolet, Butler and Wills Olds.

But it was the births that I was here to examine. My mission focused on one year: 1950, the year of my entrance into this world. It was also the year Greenfield finally had a hospital of its own. I carefully turned the pages until I reached two-thirds of the way through the year (January to August of 1950 having no special interest to me, being still in the womb at that time). I was looking for early September 1950, to either confirm or refute what I had always been told. That I was close, but no cigar—no pun intended, since cigars were surely what proud new papas were passing out back then.

Yes, I had been told that I was *almost* the first baby born in Adair County Memorial Hospital, but not quite. There would certainly have been a fuss made over this first born, a baby who could lay claim to not only being a native son—assuming a baby boy and not a baby girl—but the *very first* native son not born in either another town or at home. The first one born in the sparkling new hospital on the east end of town. There surely would have been gifts showered on the kid and the proud parents. Just because I wasn't in possession of any gifts didn't lead me to conclude I was not the first. After all, some sixty years later those gifts could have long since disappeared. I needed to find out for myself, once and for all.

Adair County Free Press, Thursday, September 7, 1950, "First Baby Born in Hospital." A picture accompanied this brief news item, a shot of a beaming mother holding her newborn baby. Now, it is common knowledge that newborn babies all look the same, with little to differentiate them. Certainly nothing revealing in a black-and-white photo from sixty-some years ago. So, my first glance at the tyke provided me no evidence. But one glance at the mother confirmed my suspicion. Close, but no cigar. She didn't look a thing like my mother. Who it *did* look like was exactly who it *was*: Delphine Jensen, holding her new baby boy, Michael Dean Jensen.

In an ironic twist, some sixteen years later Delphine and I would work for the same boss, Bernie Berg, who operated Berg's Sure Save Market on the northwest corner of the square. Delphine ran the cash register and I bagged groceries, the two of us engaging in idle chitchat as we passed the hours. I don't recall Delphine ever bringing up the subject of her delivering the first baby in the new hospital, but why would she? Folks in our town weren't the bragging sort, even if it involved such a milestone as the first baby in the new digs.

It was the closing sentence in the news item that accompanied the picture that stung the most:

"Michael Dean will receive the prizes offered by Greenfield merchants for the first baby born in the new hospital."

Like a victim picking a perpetrator out of a lineup, I had now confirmed what I had always known to be the truth but had never been able to fully accept: I wasn't first, and so I didn't get the windfall showered on number one.

Now resigned to my fate, I flipped to the next issue of the weekly:

Adair County Free Press, "Stork Notes," Thursday, September 14, 1950:

"Mr. and Mrs. Dick Porter announce the arrival of an eight pound son, Friday morning at the new hospital. Mrs. Myrtie Porter of Greenfield and William Fagan of Stuart are grandparents. He has been named Gary Allen."

Here it was, such a simple statement of a few basic facts, yet so much to reflect on. *An eight pound son.* A pretty healthy weight, especially fast forwarding fourteen years when I started high school as a scrawny, 80-pound freshman. Not a beefcake by any measure, but still more than the 6 pounds, 3 ounces registered by Michael Dean Jensen three days earlier. Maybe that was it. Maybe he beat me out because, at barely over 6 pounds, he came out early. But alas, I am resigned to the fact that the distinction was for the first baby born in the hospital, not the first one born in it weighing more than 6 pounds, 3 ounces.

Mrs. Myrtie Porter of Greenfield and William Fagan of Stuart are grandparents. Another simple statement of fact, but one I hadn't ever given that much thought to—the fact that by the time of my birth, I was already down to two grandparents. Myrtie Porter was the widow of my grandpa, John, who died the year before I was born. William Fagan, my mother's dad, had already been widowed for eighteen years, my grandmother, Ethyl Reed, having died in 1932. Two grandparents starting out. Growing up in Greenfield, I never dwelled on this deficiency, accepting it not much differently than the fact that I had two parents. It was what it was. Grandpa Fagan would be gone by the time I reached high school, and Grandma Porter just as I was finishing college.

He has been named Gary Allen. What could have been so startling about this, to see as I read the faded, yellowed pages of the *Free Press* that I had in fact been named Gary Allen? Maybe that day in the *Free Press* offices was the first time I knew my birth weight, but my name? It is the moniker I have known for all these years, so why something akin to a revelation on my part? Possibly it was something about the immediacy of it—he *has* been named Gary Allen, as if it just happened. In fact, I *had* just been named—if not on the day of my birth, at least in time for the "Stork Notes" to appear in the paper.

Friday morning at the new hospital. Not revealing that I was born in the new hospital, as I had known that all along, even if I wasn't the first. But *Friday morning.* Some folks know the day of the week they were born, but until I read my "Stork Note," I don't recall ever being told or ever doing the math myself to figure out the day of the week I was born. But, so what?

I can't pinpoint exactly why it should matter, but I am glad to be part of the fraternal order of Friday babies. Knowing the day of the week of one's birth is another way to differentiate, putting those born on a Friday in a different bucket from those born on a Thursday or other day of the week. See that 8-pound, blue-eyed, brown-haired baby over there? The lad was born on a Friday.

This raises other questions in my mind, ones I hadn't considered in all the years since that eventful day. Although the "Stork Note" doesn't give the time of day, it says I was born on Friday morning. Did the folks rush out to the hospital in the middle of the night? Or did Mom wake up Friday morning and tell Dad it was time to go? Did Dad take the day off from driving his truck route that day? Did Father Kane, himself new to town, stop by the hospital to bless the new laddie? Any celebratory toasts back at the house that night to usher me in? Was there a rush of visitors over the weekend to get a peek at the newest member of the Porter household? I am guessing that Mom, being the devout Catholic she was, missed Mass that Sunday for the first time in years.

The Adair County Memorial Hospital still stands on the east end of town, just past the intersection of State Highways 25 and 92. But coming full circle, just like in pre-1950, pregnant mothers in town now have to make a road trip. Babies are no longer delivered at the hospital. Maybe I wasn't the only 8-pound, blue-eyed, brown-haired baby ever born at that hospital on a Friday morning. But I'd bet my baby boots I was the only 8-pound, blue-eyed, brown-haired one born there on a Friday morning and given the name Gary Allen.

We are all unique in ways we may never consider.

Personal Collection

FALL FROM GRACE

School Begins Next Monday

*"The final year before the new building is ready
will see classes spilling over into three other buildings.
The kindergarten will be in the Masonic Hall. Two sections
of first grade will meet in the new basement room of the
Presbyterian Church, which has been divided by a partition.
Two sections of second grade will use the Methodist Church."*

From the *Adair County Free Press*, August 28, 1957

Dear Grace,

I have just taken another soothing sip from my early-morning coffee and glanced out the bathroom window in my room at the Hotel Greenfield. Some fifty-seven years later, and there you still stand proudly at attention, as if nothing ever happened. But you and I know better. For it was you, Grace, who stole a young lad's dignity and considerably reduced his pride...not to mention putting his arm in a sling for an extended period of time.

Trying to reach back to the second grade is no easy task for someone in their sixth decade, but let me remind you as best I can of the circumstances of our acquaintance. My compatriots and I had been shuffled around in our early school years, ending up in the basement of the Methodist church and eagerly awaiting our move to the new elementary school under construction on the north end of town. This was the church you kept a watchful eye on over the years, each Sunday carefully noting who was faithful and who was missing from the pews.

Spending an entire school year in the basement of that church you watched over was eventful, even for a young boy of seven years old. I also recall it as the year one of my life-long buddies, Sergio Kapfer, moved to town and joined us in the church basement. (You didn't know the farm kids. They didn't join us until the following year, when the new elementary was ready. A handful of those country kids you never knew have remained friends to this day: Mike Beaman, Gary Keese, and Donnie Wilson. Another buddy, Scott Chesnut, didn't come to town until the fourth grade.)

So there we were during the week, a rowdy group of rambunctious second graders, eager to explore our new surroundings. It didn't take me too long to discover you there on the north side of the church. My intention was to just introduce myself, pay you a compliment or two on your lovely branches, and be on my way before the school bell signaled the end of recess. But then you tempted me, as if you bore the fruit a latter-day Adam or Eve would find hard to resist. No, you bore no apples; but you still somehow tempted me to shinny up that first notch in your lovely trunk. *Come on up,* you teased. *Take a look at the view from up here.* So up I climbed for just one little peek. And what a glorious sight it was. Views of the town square, of the dock where my Dad's truck was kept when he wasn't driving.

But alas, recess was nearing an end, as signaled by the clanging of the school bell. Cousin Pam motioned to me that I best make my way back down to ground level, as the teacher was now rounding the corner of the church and headed in my direction. You, dear Grace, could have warned me of this turn of events and saved me from the panic that set in, both of us knowing full well I would be staying after school for this latest shenanigan. But instead, you left me hanging out there—literally, hanging. As I began to make my exit from you, one of my legs snagged in that same notch I had just used to pull myself up. My leg stayed wedged in the notch, but the upper part of my torso made a less than graceful—hence my name for you—exit from your embrace, my left shoulder leading the way.

The crunch of bony shoulder on a scrawny seven-year-old as he met the hardened ground is a sound I can remember to this day. What I can't remember is you showing any bit of remorse, let alone taking the slightest bit of responsibility for my plight. You could have come clean and explained to the teacher that it was, in fact, you who had lured me up for a quick look-see. But no, when my classmates came to peel me off the ground and haul me back to the classroom, you just looked on innocently, as if you had no part whatsoever in all of this. By this time, the teacher had called my folks to say they better come have a look at me.

From there it was a short two blocks over to Dr. Gantz's office, the same doc who just a few short years earlier had delivered me into this world. The upper arm was broken, but up too high for a cast, so just a wrap held the arm in place. Here I was with a broken arm, but not even the glory of a cast for my classmates to write good wishes on. Not to worry. I wasn't alone. That same year two other classmates broke bones: Karen Harris a leg and my buddy, Sergio, his arm!

As I take the last few sips from my morning coffee, I gaze out the window to see you still standing all these years later, sly one that you are. The Methodist church has been gone for years, replaced by the post office. Now, instead of watching over the faithful, you keep an eye out for the daily mail.

I can only hope, dear Grace, that someday you will come clean.

Postscript: On a recent trip home I drove by where the tree had stood for so many years. To my disappointment and guilt, the tree had been chopped down, reduced to nothing more than a stump. Disappointment that I wouldn't be able to snap one more picture of the scene of the crime. Guilt for all I had written, implicating the poor tree for my own foolishness. My apologies, dear Grace.

THE WHITE HOUSE
AND THE WEST WING

New Era in Education Starts Here

*"Greenfield Community School youngsters will swarm
into their class rooms Thursday to begin a new era in
education here. For the first time there will be no rural
schools operating. Grade school youngsters will be attending
classes in the handsome new building....Ended are the
years of crowded classrooms, cramped playground space,
temporary classrooms in church basements and a bus garage."*

From the *Adair County Free Press*, August 27, 1958

Well no, not *that* White House—the famous one on Pennsylvania
Avenue in our nation's capital. Nor its wing reserved for the official
business of the executive branch. The white house I refer to is the
one I grew up in—not one on an avenue, but on Dodge Street. And
the west wing I refer to is one that will soon be a passing memory,
along with the rest of Nodaway Valley Elementary School (before
consolidation, it was Greenfield Elementary). The new school is
scheduled to be open for classes this fall.

The opening of Greenfield Elementary School on the north
side of town in 1958 shortened my daily commute. I started my

academic training on the south side in Miss Huston's kindergarten class, blanket in tow. After successfully navigating our way through the first grade, my classmates and I were shuffled off to the basement of the old Methodist church, now the site of the post office. No, a new parochial school wasn't taking shape in Greenfield. The church basement was simply a convenient holding spot for us second graders until the new elementary was completed.

So my walk to the third grade was a mere two blocks from *my* white house, straight down Dodge Street to the west wing of the new elementary. And my classmates and I stayed in that west wing for the next four years, until we were off to junior high back on the south side of town. In fact, we simply worked our way up the west wing each year, from south to north. It would be foolish to think one would be able to recollect many details of events that took place nearly sixty years ago. However, I do recall the names of some of our teachers during those four years: White, Parker, Pickrell, Finck, Sheriff, Swanson, and Killion were among those who reminded us this was all *elementary.*

The breezeway separated the two wings of the elementary. We traveled over to the east side on a daily basis, including trips to the cafeteria for lunch. Two things stick out to me about the cafeteria: getting your meal card punched for lunch and using a straw to drink milk out of a carton. Another recollection is that you didn't wash up in a normal sink before lunch. Instead, you stood at a semi-circular, trough-like basin and drew water by tapping your foot down on a rubber ring. Whether this device was a very early attempt at water conservation by the school, I can't say.

Adjacent to the cafeteria was the "multi-purpose" room, one of its main purposes being Phys. Ed classes during cold weather. One game contested in this room, with its massive wall of windows on the east side, stands out among all others. It went by the name of "battleball" or "dodgeball"—take your pick. Officially, the object of the game was to throw the ball at an opponent on the other side, and in so doing tag him or her out. But truth be told, the real objective was to see how large a welt you could apply to the exposed thigh of an opponent, courtesy of that menacing red ball that was just shy of being hard as a baseball. When the weather permitted, we took our aggressions outside to the tetherball courts. Maybe not quite as dangerous as battleball, but still a game that took some quick reflexes to avoid being decapitated by a rope tethered to a ball coming at you at high speed.

Another room on the east side of the elementary was one you wanted to avoid at all costs. Across from the cafeteria was the principal's office. Our school wasn't big enough for an assistant principal, so if you had any disciplinary issues you saw *the* principal, Mr. Jochumsen. There was no upside if your teacher sent you down to see the principal. From the slightest of infractions—such as running down the hallways one too many times—to more serious offenses—such as skipping school—you did your best to avoid being summoned to Mr. J's office. But as I said before, it would be foolish to think I could recollect many details from nearly sixty years ago!

Sadly, my old white house on Dodge Street was torn down a few years ago. Soon the familiar single-story, red-brick building with the flat-top roof, including its west wing, will share that same fate. But the memories will remain, for it was where so many of us learned our three Rs. And the place where we learned how to dodge a ball, duck a rope, and avoid a trip to see Mr. J.

This essay appeared in the *Adair County Free Press* on June 14, 2017.

ENCYCLOPEDIAS
AND GOLF CLUBS

"The arrival of the wonderful new
ENCYCLOPEDIA AMERICANA in your
home is a truly memorable event in your life."

From the brochure that accompanied
The Encyclopedia Americana, 1959 Edition

As I was sitting one day in the lower level of our house, I glanced up to the bookshelves to see a handsome set of encyclopedias—a dinosaur from the dark ages, B.G. (Before Google). They reminded me of a set of golf clubs I no longer have.

Say what? What sort of an imagination does it take to associate dusty old reference books with tools used to hit a white ball around an open field?

There is only one explanation. If memory serves me, both the books and the clubs came to me from one of the locals in town. And since I still have the encyclopedias but not the golf clubs, I am guessing the former was a purchase and the latter a loan from the local.

Our family straddled the fence, sometimes literally as well as figuratively. We straddled many a fence at the various horse shows we frequented around the state. However, we weren't farmers. I truly was a town kid. But make no mistake about it, by no means were we members of the country club set either.

Most of the members of the country club out on the west side of town were professionals. That is to say they wore slacks to work rather than jeans or overalls. Doctors (there were just three), dentists, lawyers, insurance men, some of the merchants up on the town square—these were the folks who made up the membership of the Greenfield Country Club.

The farmers didn't belong to the country club. In the summer, they needed to cultivate the fields, milk the cows, and slop the pigs. No time for whacking a little white dimpled ball around an open field. Neither were the town folks who labored with their hands for a living part of this fraternity. They came home from work too exhausted for such frivolity.

One summer when I was home from college, I decided to try the game of golf. The country club was offering a special summer membership. With the loan of a set of clubs, off I went. I didn't start by caddying to familiarize myself with the finer points of the game. Nor did I take lessons. I didn't join a foursome of guys my age and talk hoops, girls, and music. No, I was on my own. It must have been the same personality trait that drew me to accounting and long-distance running. What an oddball, dragging my set of borrowed golf clubs around the course, solitary sort that I was. But that is what I did a couple times a week that one summer. I played a few times after I graduated from college, but I never got the urge to take up the sport on a serious basis.

It has been pointed out to me that in today's digital world my thirty-volume set of *The Encyclopedia Americana* is nothing but a dust-collector. Dump them and move on, I am told. But I don't see that happening. They are too much a link to the past. The encyclopedias are what allowed me to explore the world, without ever leaving home. I really had no burning desire to leave Greenfield, but I did want to explore. The encyclopedias allowed me to do just that. As the brochure said, their arrival in your home was a memorable event!

These days, if you want to find out something, you use your fingers to touch the screen on a "smart" phone, not to turn the pages of a book. Before you know it, you have the answer to your question about the capital of Tanzania, literally at your fingertips. Problem is, by tomorrow not only have you forgotten the capital of Tanzania, you have no recollection whatsoever of why you wanted to know it in the first place. Not so with a bound set of encyclopedias. You read something in them and it sticks with you.

Allow me to illustrate. I pull Volume 27 from the shelf, intrigued by the spine that indicates it contains everything you ever wanted to know from "Trance to Venial Sin." I am told that the former is "a state in which the voluntary functions of the body are suspended and in which a dream life is carried on of more coherency than in ordinary sleep." The last page in Volume 27 is a reminder of my religious upbringing—venial sin is "a term used to signify the lesser transgressions of the law of God or of the church, in contradistinction to mortal sin…" Now it comes back to me. Limit the number of venial sins, stay away from the mortal variety, and you could keep the number of Our Fathers and Hail Marys reasonable next Saturday in the confessional.

Encyclopedias and golf clubs. One takes you on all sorts of adventures without ever leaving home, maybe as far away as Tanzania. Puts you in a trance and reminds you that there is a difference between venial and mortal sins. The other frustrates you until you hit that one perfect shot that keeps you coming back for more. And if I remember right, the language resulting from a less-than-perfect shot only counts as a venial sin.

CLASS OF '68

*"The Class of 1968 received their diplomas in
an outdoor commencement program at the
athletic field. The setting had the green beauty of an
Iowa May, but the air had a chill reminiscent of winter."*

From *Black and Gold*, the Greenfield High
School student newspaper, May 24, 1968

For my fellow GHS Tigers:

When you are a bean-counter, numbers are always rattling around in your head. Similar to the way you keep hearing the melody of your favorite song from our senior year of high school… just not quite as soothing.

Fifty years ago, sixty-two members of the GHS class of 1968 walked out of that red-brick rectangular building on the left-hand side of this picture for the last time, ready to conquer the world. The year was one of the most monumental in the history of our country: assassinations, killings in a far-off land, riots in the streets back home, moon shots. Four years earlier, we finished junior high and made the short walk from that square edifice on the right-hand side of the picture to the high school. (Maybe I didn't master the isosceles triangle in our geometry class, but I do remember the difference between a square and a rectangle.)

More numbers: 1950, the year most of us were born, the midpoint of the twentieth century. Being born in that year has always made the math easy. It is now 2018, so subtract 1950 and guess what? The members of the class of '68 are all turning 68!

We town kids began our formal education as kindergartners in the fall of 1955 at the old junior high building. (It wasn't until third grade that the farm boys and girls left their one-room schoolhouses and joined us in the big city.) We drug our blankets, Linus-like, to meet our very first teachers: Mrs. Weller and Miss Huston.

As it played out over the years, our class became nomads, wandering up and down the streets of Greenfield. By second grade, we had been shuffled off to the basement of the old Methodist church, on the site that is now home to the post office. This move didn't signal the start of a new parochial school in town and a conversion of every one of the Catholics, Lutherans, and Presbyterians to the teachings of John Wesley. No, we had been sent there as construction progressed on the new elementary school out on the northern edge of town.

The new school was ready for all of us renegades in the fall of 1958. What a magnificent new structure it was, complete with a breezeway, a cafeteria, a music room, a gym (games of battleball could be brutal), and outdoor courts for the wondrous game of tetherball. We spent four years together in that building. Each of us can probably recall the names of some of our teachers from those years: White, Parker, Pickrell, Finck, Sheriff, Swanson, Killion, and a few others all had a hand in our early education. Some were "Miss," others "Missus," but always of the female persuasion. No "Misters" for us.

When it came time to enter that scary realm called junior high, we were sent packing back to the original scene of the crime: the old two-story block building on the south side of town. Each of us can probably remember certain events from those two years: our first time with a homeroom, moving from one class to the next, and team sports. Certainly everyone can picture the exact room they were sitting in on November 22, 1963. We were eighth graders when Mr. Nolan delivered the news and we were sent home early to huddle by our television sets to watch the events in Dallas unfold. If my memory isn't failing me, I recall stopping off at the Fees' house on the way home.

In the fall of 1964, we began the four years that most clearly define us as the class of '68. Greenfield High School, before the Tigers went the way of the dinosaur and were replaced by the Nodaway Valley Wolverines. We left the security of the old block building and found ourselves rookies as we roamed the long hallways of the high school, trying to figure out where our lockers and classrooms were located. The Beatles had just invaded America, and we were at that age when we were at least starting to think, *I wanna hold your hand*, about someone of the opposite sex. Maybe get up enough courage to buy a corsage and ask her to the homecoming dance.

And what a homecoming it was in 1967, one for the ages. It seems the senior boys took the tradition of bringing an outhouse to town for the bonfire a bit too far. The truck belonging to the father of one of these boys (I won't say who) was seen hauling one too many privies for the likes of the principal. So ended the tradition...but what a roaring bonfire it was that year!

We all have our favorite memories. For some it may be the sports teams and their tutors: Coach Matthews for football, Coach Hall for basketball, and Coach Riley for wrestling. And Mrs. May for tennis, that one-and-only girls' sport.

And then there were groups like Hi-Y, Y-Teens, GRA, and FFA. There was also all manner of singing and playing going on: girls' glee, boys' glee, swing choir, mixed chorus, and marching band. The thespians among us took on the senior class play. Did it not take some fine acting to pull off *Get Smart* as if we weren't already pretty intelligent?

Maybe even a few of those memories are from the classroom: dissecting frogs in biology, figuring out how to use a slide rule in Mr. Cook's class, learning to count to ten (at best) in Spanish, or mastering the nearly dead art of taking shorthand. For me it was under the brilliant tutelage of Mr. Gibson that I began my life-long love affair with debits, credits, and the double-entry system of accounting.

Each of us also has memories outside those hallowed halls. Maybe it is dancing at the old 4-H building to "G-L-O-R-I-A." Stopping in the bowling alley on a Friday night for a cheeseburger and curly fries. And then, depending on the time *on* the clock, cruising the square clockwise, rather than in the prescribed counterclockwise fashion.

Looking back, living as we did in the insulated world of high school seniors, how could we have known what a historical year 1968 would turn out to be? In April, as we prepared to graduate, we read the *Des Moines Register* account of the assassination of Martin Luther King. In May, each of us crossed the stage as *The Graduate* while Simon and Garfunkel sang their ode to "Mrs. Robinson." In June, already working on our tans, we listened on the radio to a report that Bobby Kennedy had been gunned down in an L.A. hotel. By the end of summer, we went our separate ways, some off to college, others to join up with Uncle Sam, others to start a family. Archie Bell and the Drells, from Houston, Texas, told us that it was time to "Tighten Up." Our age of innocence was over.

Some call Greenfield home, while others rarely get back. We are scattered across the country, from D.C. to Seattle. But there will always be that common bond amongst us. Because fifty years ago in May, each of us crossed that stage, forever binding us together as the GHS Class of '68.

Oh, and that favorite melody I can't get out of my head? Must be that I was and still am a daydream believer. But it wasn't Sleepy Jean. Our homecoming queen that year was Janet Lillie.

A version of this essay was read at the GHS Class of '68 forty-year reunion and appeared in the *Adair County Free Press* on August 6, 2008.

Personal Collection

SUNSET AT LOUCKS GROVE

"Being near the church was important to the pioneers even after their death. Loucks Grove Church was built one-quarter mile east of Loucks Grove Cemetery. There is a beautiful view of the cradle-to-grave church from the hilltop of the cemetery."

From *One Hundred Years Loucks Grove Church, 1895-1995*

The dust from the gravel road hangs in the air like chalk from a teacher's blackboard. The roar from the car's air conditioner makes it hard to hear anything else. But soon we are parked and left with the serenity of the Iowa countryside on a summer's eve just before sunset. To be specific, these are the rolling hills of Adair County—the next one over from Madison, with its famous covered bridges.

My wife and I are on one of our pilgrimages to visit the final resting place of my great-grandparents and a few other assorted relatives. Loucks Grove is the "Cemetery That Time Forgot," miles from the modern one in the county seat of Greenfield. As best as can be determined, no one has been buried in this country cemetery for forty years. Still plenty of room for anyone who cares to join the souls now at rest here.

Loucks Grove sits on a grassy hilltop with views to the south and the east that stretch for miles on end. Alternating fields of corn and soybeans are laid out with the precision of a patchwork quilt on the fertile landscape. Looking from this vantage point to the east you can't help but focus on the modest white church that sits on the main road, a few hundred yards down the hill. Simple black lettering above the door and under the steeple proclaims that this is "Loucks Grove Church, A.D. 1895."

Back on the hilltop, the cemetery is enclosed on the north and west sides by a stand of oak and elm trees in their finest summer greenery—a stand of trees that tells you this really *is* a grove. A chorus of birds sings an unknown melody in the woods, beyond which lies a meandering stream known simply as Middle River. Because it is early July, the sun peeks through a spot in the very northwest corner of the grove of trees, patiently waiting to set on another day. But before daylight runs out, there are respects to be paid. We walk softly toward the graves, over patches of white clover and brilliant emerald grass that make a fitting carpet for this living room for the deceased.

David Porter, 1851–1925

Anna Porter, 1866–1930

My great-grandparents rest under the shade of a solitary pine tree. David, fifteen years his wife's senior and gone from this life five years before her. Now they lay side by side, in a place where time no longer counts for anything.

Wesley R. Julian

Died Sept. 16, 1907

Aged 69 years, 11 months

Nancy Julian

Died December 8, 1909

Aged 68 years, 2 days

These are Anna's parents, buried next to their daughter and son-in-law, just out of the shade of the pine tree. Our family's collective memory says that the Julians' farmhouse was just down the lane from this pasture-turned-cemetery. Such a short distance to travel on the day of one's final journey in this life.

Jacob P. Kinkennon

Pvt. Co. E 47th Iowa Inf.

1820–1864

The dates stand out for obvious reasons. Though the last name isn't familiar, there is an immediate intimacy that comes from seeing the gravestone of a soldier who fought in the War Between the States. At forty-some years of age, Jacob was older than many of the young lads who marched off to help squelch the Rebellion, as Lincoln called it. Was he married? Any children left behind? Did he die in battle? Did the neighbors come and grieve Private Kinkennon when he came home for the last time?

Time is running out—not for these permanent residents, but for us visitors as the sun begins to set. Not to worry, though, as fireflies take over the work of the sun. They are serenaded by crickets who, almost on cue, begin their familiar chirping. A gentle breeze feels cool on the back of the neck as we say good-night to the residents of Loucks Grove.

Rest well.

Courtesy of The Sidey Collection®

HIGH ATOP A HILL

*"Lest we forget in this time of international crisis the
price that has already been paid for our freedom, here is
a reminder for Monday's Memorial Day service at the
Greenfield Cemetery, as Greenfield Legionnaires decorate
the crosses symbolic of our fallen soldiers in past wars."*

From the *Adair County Free Press*, June 1, 1960

The rural Iowa landscape is dotted with bucolic country cemeteries like Loucks Grove. And then every small town has a cemetery of its own. It usually sits high on a hill, keeping a watchful eye on the town below. Ours has one on the south side of town, just beyond the city limits. No fancy name—it is simply the Greenfield Cemetery.

There was a time when nearly all the town folks ended up there. They stayed close to home their entire lives, the few exceptions being those who spent time in the service of their country. Some of those who did answer the call ended up on the hill overlooking town at much too young an age. Starting with my generation, more and more of those raised in town moved away, choosing higher-paying jobs and a "better" life. I was one of them, and it is doubtful I will end up buried in the Greenfield Cemetery.

Some towns have a separate resting place for the Catholics, or some other denomination heavily represented in town. Greenfield has no separate place, even though there is a sizeable population of Catholic families. Our cemetery is very integrated—you can walk down a row interspersed with Methodists, Lutherans, Presbyterians, and Catholics.

Greenfield honors its war veterans every year on Memorial Day. Old-timers still call it by its descriptive name: Decoration Day, the day to honor the dead by placing flowers on their graves.

Take your pick as far as the name. Memorial Day or Decoration Day at the cemetery was magical in my youth. School was out for the year and summer was on the horizon. We would sit attentively on the banks of the sunken garden while the legionnaires solemnly marched along, some carrying rifles, others flags. In this essay's picture, my Uncle Max is the one in the front row on the left, with my dad directly behind him. Both of them served in the European Theatre in WWII. Uncle Max came home with shrapnel in his leg as a painful reminder of his time overseas.

Flowers were placed on the grave of the Unknown Soldier. We would wait patiently as a minister or some other dignitary delivered the Memorial Day address. The legionnaires would fire their guns off into the horizon, followed by the mournful sound of "Taps" being played off in the distance. Once the men had turned and marched back out of the garden, the sprint was on. We would race down the banks to collect the spent shells from the rifles, which the veterans took back to the Legion Hall to be "oiled." Only after I reached a less impressionistic age did I realize "oiling the guns" was code for a well-deserved shot of whiskey or a beer before joining the family for the holiday picnic.

I love walking the rows of gravestones at the cemetery. Most members of my parents' and grandparents' generations now reside there. It is while walking the rows that I recollect so much about growing up in Greenfield. Why, over there lie Ernest and Sarah Funke. So says the gravestone, but to me they will always be known by their nickname and middle name, respectively: Pete and Corrine, our neighbors two doors down. On down the row are Don and Phyllis Porter, my dad's oldest brother and his wife. Don milked cows for a living, and he and I were best buddies when I was a youngster. And down another row a bronze military plaque marks the grave of my Grandpa Fagan, a veteran of WWI.

This place is now home to so many people from my days as a town kid. They rest peacefully on the hill overlooking the place most of them never left. Greenfield was their home in life, and the cemetery high atop the hill on the edge of town is their home forevermore.

Courtesy of The Sidey Collection®

FAIRGROUNDS

*"Final preparations for the opening of the 68th
annual Adair County Fair were in full swing this week.*

*"Just 10 days remain until the fair events begin.
Monday, July 27, is entry day, but the program actually
begins the evening before when the Adair County Fair
Horse and Pony Show is held in front of the grandstand
under sponsorship of the Adair County Saddle Club....*

*"The Bill Riley Talent Show will be the top entertainment
feature on the Monday program, and Fair Secretary Helen
Porter announced there still is room for some more entries."*

From the *Adair County Free Press*, July 15, 1964

The old boy nudges me softly with his muzzle. Gentle, but still
insistent that he and I make one final tour of the fairgrounds,
which has been his home off and on over his twenty-five-plus
years. Sparky is of the earth now—no longer on it—but that won't
deter him this day. He gives a whinny.

Okay, boy. Off we go. Let's take a ride.

No need for a saddle, I slide effortlessly onto Sparky's back,
pressing my legs tightly against his warm belly. No need for a
bridle, either. The bay pony knows the way in his sleep from our

home on Dodge Street out to the Adair County Fairgrounds on the east side of town.

We start out slowly, but before long Sparky picks up the pace, breaking into a trot as we approach the entrance to the grounds. We follow a chalky gravel road around to the north side and pull alongside a finely manicured lawn, a cluster of old oak trees providing a canopy from the hot July sun. Toward the back of the lawn is a small, rectangular, white frame building with a sign on the front: Secretary's Office. A cheery young woman greets us, sticking her head out the window.

Well hello there, young buckaroo. What can I do for you this fine morning?

This here, Mrs. Secretary, is the finest pony in the county. Enter us, if you please, in the Western Pleasure Class, 14.2 hands and under. Yeah, I know he is pushing it, but trust me. He comes in just under the limits. We had his hooves shaved just yesterday.

Madam Secretary gives me a wink. She needs no convincing. She knows this bay pony better than anyone.

Helen Porter may be the one who runs this fair, but she is also my mother and the one who taught me how to ride Sparky. *It's all in your legs, Gar. Sit up in the saddle now, eyes straight ahead.* We are on her home ground, the place where she is the maestro: the conductor for the Adair County Fair, one of the finest in the state of Iowa. She hires the carnival, books the acts for the grandstand, referees all manner of disputes, and prays for good weather during the fickle summers of the Midwest.

She also hires the summer help, the fortunate few kids who get to spend their summer basking in the radiant sunshine, working on their tans, and picking up some spending cash along the way.

Call it what you will, nepotism is alive and well at the Adair County Fairgrounds. It is what gave me a summer job—mowing, painting, and sprucing up the place—leading up to the four-day July run. After the crowds went home, there were always a few more days on my time card for walking the grounds, poking a stick with a nail on the end to retrieve snow cone cups, popcorn bags, and cotton candy wrappers.

Our registration in tonight's horse show secure, I bid adieu to the secretary and point Sparky toward the cluster of livestock buildings. I glance back to the window in the office and see just the fading outline of the young woman's smiling face.

Hey, Spark, let's go check out your old stall in the horse barn. I'll give you a good brushing with the curry comb. You'll be the most handsome pony those judges ever saw!

Sparky knows the way. Just down the hill from the secretary's office is the barn where we stabled him and Mom's high-stepping American Saddle horses for much of the year. The barn smells of ripe manure, fresh hay, and oats—a pleasing mix of aromas to a boy raised around horses. I walk Sparky up and down the aisles as he whinnies greetings to the stately Clydesdales, the docile quarter horses, and the spirited Shetland ponies munching hay in their stalls.

After giving Spark that promised brushing, I climb back aboard and we continue on our way to the cattle barn. A Hereford bull stands at attention, a young 4-H boy admiring his prized possession and dreaming of a Grand Champion ribbon. Down the next aisle, a black-and-white Holstein waits patiently for her next milking. She swats the flies from her rear end, her bristly tail moving rhythmically like a metronome, keeping time to the beat of country music coming from a portable radio hanging on one of the stalls. The old gal's back haunches are so pronounced and straight you could set the supper table on them. On down the row, a Jersey turns her head toward us and flashes her saucer-like brown eyes our way, a picture of contentment. As if trying to produce a similar effect, a teenaged blonde with baby-blue eyes teases a young lad adorned in his blue-and-gold corduroy FFA jacket.

There are still fat hogs, squawking chickens, and woolly sheep to check out, but I am distracted now from making passes through any of the other barns. The aroma of greasy cheeseburgers grilling at one of the church stands fills the air. Fried onions, relish, and catsup are tempting, but suddenly I hear a voice coming from the loudspeaker in front of the grandstand. A cheeseburger washed down with a Dr. Pepper will have to wait.

I listen carefully and hear the call. *Ladies and gentlemen, will you please welcome into the ring the Western Pleasure ponies, 14.2 and under.*

I give Sparky a gentle nudge in his hindquarters, and he breaks into a fast trot as we approach the show ring in front of the grandstand. I suddenly realize we are both ill-equipped for this. I have neither cowboy hat nor boots. Sparky has neither bridle nor saddle. But it won't matter today. Expecting to hear applause from a packed crowd, I glance to my right and see an empty grandstand. Its rows of bleachers no longer sport the brightly colored green-and-white paint job I gave them every year before the fair started its run. I turn away from the grandstand to check out our competition, but there is none. I sit atop my trusted pony not in a show ring, but in a pasture of overgrown grass.

Growing antsy, Sparky seems intent on taking a lap around the old half-mile oval track. I grab hold of his mane, reminding him that I am not a young jockey on his three-year-old thoroughbred, but rather an aging cowboy atop his old bay pony. But on this day the aging cowboy and his pony have nowhere to run. The finely manicured dirt track that was once the centerpiece of the fairgrounds is now a mixture of weeds and stubble. The lonely backstretch, the wide turn leading to the long straightaway finish in front of the grandstand...

They exist only in my imagination.

Off in the distance, I hear a carney barking out his enticement: *Three balls for a dollar. Come on in, knock over the milk bottles, and win your sweetie a teddy bear.* As the sun sets off in the western sky, I see the bright lights of the Ferris wheel over the top of the grandstand and hear the *clankety-clank-clank* of the roller coaster.

I point Sparky toward the midway, eager to take in the sights and sounds of the carnival. First, I can make a pass by the church stand and grab that cheeseburger. But when I round the corner from the grandstand, the church stand is gone and the aroma of grilling burgers no longer fills the air. Where the midway once stood is an empty field. The only sound is that of a few crickets serenading us off in the distance.

I think we better start for home, old boy.

As we make our way back down the gravel road, the 4-H building comes into view. The teen dance is in full gear, and the big rolling door is all the way up to provide some relief from the hot summer evening. I hear the lyrics to "Cherish" as a local band does its best imitation of The Association. I turn my bay pony toward home, realizing now that I will forever cherish my memories of summers spent at the old fairgrounds.

Personal Collection

1,252 SQUARE FEET

"Large 3 bedroom home located in a great neighborhood.
It features open floor plan, huge bathrooms,
bedrooms and kitchen. Large living room.
Needs work but priced accordingly. Won't last long."

From realtor's listing for 205 NE Dodge Street,
Greenfield, Iowa, November 21, 2014

On a recent trip home, I couldn't resist the temptation. It is one my wife, Melissa, warns me about each time we are in town. But like Adam and Eve, I can never seem to resist one small bite from the apple. The apple in this case is a swing by the old homestead at 205 NE Dodge Street. The reason for her warning is that a mere passing by the house where I grew up never fails to bring some sadness and disappointment. Nothing is ever quite the way you remember it.

Alone on this trip home, and thus without Melissa's reminder, I waste no time pulling up in front of my house. Not only did the old, two-story, white frame house look forlorn, something appeared in the front yard I never expected to see: a realtor's sign. Homes go up for sale all the time, so why should I have been so shocked to see a sign in the yard of a ninety-year-old house?

Maybe I'm alone in thinking this way, but you just don't expect your childhood home to be a commodity up for sale.

Dad came home from WWII, worked a few years, married Mom, and then signed a note for a loan. He gave the note to his mother to buy the house and started a family. The house stayed in the family for the next fifty years, until Dad could no longer make it up and down the flight of stairs to the only bathroom. He sold it and now it was up for sale again. For me, the realtor's sign was a strange juxtaposition, no more fitting the landscape than if a palm tree had been planted on this Iowa lawn. Yet there it was.

A second temptation arose as soon as I returned home to Wisconsin. In this case, Adam's apple was the internet. Barely in the front door, I was online and checking out the realtor's listing. Piece of cake. Google "205 NE Dodge, Greenfield, Iowa" and up pops the "property details." My home has become a *property*.

Large 3 bedroom home located in a great neighborhood.

I didn't grow up in a three-bedroom home. We had two upstairs bedrooms, one for our parents and the other shared by me and my brother. (I heard later that a third bedroom had been carved out of the downstairs living room.) Back then, any heat on the second floor came from a space heater. Before global warming, during those brutal Midwestern winters enough ice formed on the windows in our bedroom to allow for a lively game of tic-tac-toe.

Located in a great neighborhood.

Mind you, I considered our part of town on the north side of Greenfield a neighborhood. But great? This would imply some sections of town were more or less desirable than others. I never thought of it that way. We had the swimming pool across the street, the Catholic church a block away, the city park another block to the south. Maybe these made for a great neighborhood. I don't know.

It features open floor plan, huge bathrooms, bedrooms and kitchen. Large living room.

I don't recall anything colossal about our bathroom, singular as it was. Big enough for one person to attend to a few daily rituals, the next in line waiting patiently in the narrow hallway. And if my mother were still alive, she might take issue with the description of her kitchen as "huge." Big enough for her to turn from the sink to the stove, whip the mashed potatoes, turn the chicken frying on the other burner, reach below to check on the cherry pie in the oven, and swing around to the stand-up freezer to pull out some frozen peas.

Large living room. Large enough to accommodate the alternating boxing and wrestling matches we staged in this room. Not so large that you couldn't yell, "Out of bounds," after being pinned into the corner after a vicious left hook. Just be careful, Dad would warn, not to back into that new Zenith behind you. Money doesn't grow on trees, you know.

Open floor plan? As if our house had been featured in *Architectural Digest*, a home suitable for today's way of living. Granted, there was no wall separating the living room from the dining room. If the dining room table wasn't set up for company (the only time we ate in this room), it doubled as our own private basketball court...half court that is. A cottage cheese carton was tacked to a plastered beam that separated the dining room from the living room and a tennis ball served as surrogate for a basketball. Thanks to that stylish "open" floor plan, you could spill over into the living room after a particularly hard drive to the basket without crashing into a wall.

Also included in the listing was some legalese about anyone in any way connected to a certain bank being strictly prohibited from buying the old homestead. The bank mentioned, the one that now owned my house, was one of the ten largest banks in the world! My guess is that it would probably not break this bank if it had to accept less than full asking price.

Under the property details were some interesting statistics. Lot size: 8,712 square feet. My math tells me our house and yard sat on about a fifth of an acre. So nowhere near an acre, but plenty big for a vegetable garden, a couple cherry trees, and a lively game of home run derby. And then there was the garage out back with a hoop attached over the door for practicing free throws and jump shots.

Yet it was the other square footage number that most caught my attention: 1,252. Without ever before giving it the slightest thought, I now knew, courtesy of the internet, that I had grown up in a house that measured 1,252 square feet. I only became aware of square footage when Melissa and I bought our first house. Before that, I had no context for knowing what was big and what was small.

I doubt when Dad bought the house from his mother that he queried her on its dimensions. And all I knew was that the house had a bedroom for Mom and Dad, one for the boys, a living room for watching *Gunsmoke* and *Leave It to Beaver*, a kitchen for Mom to cook in and us to eat in, and a dining room for half-court basketball.

What more could a young kid want?

Personal Collection

TEARDOWN

*"Teardown; noun: A building bought
solely for the purpose of demolishing."*

From google.com

Melissa and I were home for a family wedding, my cousin Jacque's granddaughter. It was Jacque who broke the news outside St. John's after the ceremony. The old house at 205 NE Dodge had been torn down. She certainly had fond memories of her cousins' house, growing up herself just around the corner on the other side of the pool.

Jacque had taken pictures of the house before it was demolished. The pictures were like a slow-moving video reel, showing the regression from a house intact, to one without windows, and then a bulldozer in the yard ready to do its work.

Now I am told there is no house at all. Just an empty lot.

The house I had grown up in, where I lived for the first eighteen years of my life, was a *teardown*. Back then, I am fairly certain the term did not exist, at least not in Greenfield. Certainly not as a noun. Someone might *tear* (v.) down an old house, but the dignity of the structure wasn't called into question by giving it the name "teardown." Even when the term came into popular usage, it normally referred to an older home sitting on a very expensive piece of real estate—say one along the north shore of Lake Michigan outside Chicago. Not a house in a small rural town.

Pictures aside, I needed to see for myself. There was enough time before the wedding reception out at the fairgrounds to swing by and take a look.

The old saying goes, "If only these walls could talk." But there were no walls anymore—or for that matter, any windows, roof, or chimney. I stared at a blank canvas, as a painter would, looking and waiting for that moment of inspiration. I tried to recollect all the happy times and the not-so-happy ones that took place in the house that once stood on this blank canvas.

The time we got a miniature pool table for Christmas, setting it up right there in the dining room.

The first time we realized our old beagle, Ralph, was blind, finding him under the kitchen table, sitting up, begging for scraps.

The Sunday night my buddy, Curt Weber, and I sat in the living room to watch Jim Morrison and The Doors on the Ed Sullivan Show. *Dad marching up the stairs in disgust at their outrageous behavior.*

The wintry night the exhaust from a portable space heater iced over, sending all four of us out on the snowy front lawn to regain our senses, narrowly avoiding a front-page headline in the Free Press: *"Local Family Succumbs to Deadly Fumes."*

The time after college graduation when I loaded up my Ford Falcon in the backyard, heading off to Denver to conquer the world.

The day I brought my girlfriend, Melissa, home from Colorado to meet the family, them all wondering if at the ripe old age of twenty-six I would ever get married. We did, less than two years later.

I look for the sidewalk that ran from the street to the front porch. But it is gone as well. All that remains are two trees, one in the front on the right side of the lot and the other on the left side. The two trees stand sentinel. *Any trespassers beware: We are watching you.*

I see a garage in the backyard, but it is one that was added much later. The old garage with the orange basketball hoop attached to its door has been gone for many years. I also see the bulldozer, meant to destroy any evidence that a family once lived here. It did its work well.

For the longest time after that weekend I kept staring at the pictures. The house still standing intact, although with a realtor's sign in the front yard. The house standing, but with its windows removed. A big piece of equipment standing in the front lawn, ready to do its destructive work.

Now, all I see before me is an empty lot.

Yes, my house was a teardown. Pure economics. Run the numbers, do a bit of analysis. Even factoring in the cost to demolish it, the property was worth more *without* the house than *with* it.

Dad came home from the war, a young kid in his mid-twenties. A few short years later, he met the woman he would marry, my mom. The newlyweds needed a place to start their lives together, and so they bought the house from his mother, my grandmother. Both of my folks, now deceased. What would their reaction be to this, to the demise of the house they raised their family in, lived in together up until the day my mother died?

A few months later, it struck me. Why had it taken me so long to sort it all out? To make sense of it all? A house can be torn down. Windows can be taken out, walls knocked down, concrete removed. But what can't be torn down is a *home*.

You don't look at pictures to see your home. The only way to see it is to close your eyes. That's how you see your boyhood home, how you see the beagle begging under the kitchen table. It's how you feel his soft, floppy ears as you scratch behind one of them. How you smell Mom's cherry pie baking in the oven. How you taste that cherry pie with a scoop of homemade ice cream on the top. How you hear Jim Morrison "lighting your fire" in the living room. The *senses* remind you of home, not pictures on a phone.

It's not just my house that is gone. So are many of the buildings from my youth. The old junior high building on the other side of town was torn down years ago, a grocery store now standing in its place. But when I close my eyes, I don't see a store. I see a basement locker room where we suited up for football games. I smell analgesic balm. I hear Coach rallying the troops for a Friday-night battle with Mount Ayr.

The old horse barn at the fairgrounds was demolished long ago. But in my mind, I swing open the big wooden door and stroll down the aisle. Sparky pushes his nose against the gate on his stall, whinnying to greet me. The aromas of freshly mown hay and ripe manure fill the air, two essentials in the life of a horse.

The church where the family wedding was held occupies the very spot where the old St. John's Catholic Church sat. When I close my eyes, I see Father Kane, the old Irish priest. I smell the incense burning. I taste the chalky communion wafers.

Now I am back home, strolling the streets of Greenfield.

A town kid once more.

ACKNOWLEDGMENTS

How do you thank an entire town? It was the nurturing environment I had growing up in Greenfield that made this book a reality. So I'd like to give heartfelt thanks to all my family and friends—some still living, others since passed—for helping me create these memories.

For as long as I can remember, reading the *Adair County Free Press* has been a weekly ritual. Thanks to the generations of the Sidey family for reporting on and preserving the history of our town. From the beginning, my vision was to match my essays with the striking black-and-white photos from The Sidey Collection®. Linda Sidey, Ed's widow, has painstakingly helped me find just the right photo to accompany many of the essays. Thanks, Linda, for all your support and encouragement along the way. Cindy Sidey Buck, Hugh's daughter, has been a champion for this project from the beginning and graciously wrote the Foreword.

Thank you to both the *Adair County Free Press* and the *River Falls Journal* for first printing some of the essays in this collection. And to Roleen Chiles, Jacque Eblen, Louise Pierce, and John Porter for other pictures that appear in the book. Glad to have found Jason Schrank at Flashback Film & Video Transfer. In Greenfield, thank you to Ed & Eva's, The Corner, and the

Greenfield Public Library for hosting readings. The old issues of the *Adair County Free Press* at the library were invaluable in doing my research—thanks to Library Director Lynn Heinbuch for her guidance.

A few years ago, I took classes at The Loft Literary Center in Minneapolis on writing about your hometown. Thanks to Roxanne Sadovsky and my fellow writers for their support in the early stages. Paulette Alden at the University of Minnesota led a workshop that provided more reinforecement. John Potter, Executive Director, and the staff at The Phipps Center for the Arts in Hudson, Wisconsin, created a welcoming environment for much of my writing. And a shout-out to Chapter2Books for supporting local authors. Thanks also to fellow writer Carol Bodensteiner for her encouragement along the way.

My publisher—the Write Place in Pella, Iowa—has been the perfect partner to bring this book to completion. Thanks to Sarah Purdy, editor extraordinaire, for her meticulous attention to detail. And to Michelle Stam for a masterful job in designing the cover and interior of the book.

When we first met, I was the kid from a small town and Melissa the girl from Detroit. Melissa has embraced Greenfield and its people since the first time she visited. And she is the one who kept reminding me that there were stories to be told and that I should be the one to tell them. It is fitting that publication of this book coincides with our fortieth anniversary. Her love and support over these forty years are what made these stories worth telling.

ABOUT THE AUTHOR

Gary Porter grew up in Greenfield, Iowa. He graduated from Drake University, where he is currently a Distinguished Lecturer. Gary lives in Hudson, Wisconsin, with his wife, Melissa, and their rescue dog, Polly. He is the author of numerous accounting textbooks and *Duffy: The Tale of a Terrier*, a book inspired by the couple's first shelter dog.

CPSIA information can be obtained
at www.ICGtesting.com
Printed in the USA
BVHW051950090320
574544BV00014B/507

9 780999 488782